KEEN

KARL D. KEEN

Author's Tranquility Press
ATLANTA, GEORGIA

KARL D. KEEN/Author's Tranquility Press
3800 Camp Creek Pkwy SW Bldg. 1400-116 #1255
Atlanta, GA 30331, USA
www.authorstranquilitypress.com

Ordering Information:
Quantity sales. Special discounts are available on quantity purchases by corporations, associations, and others. For details, contact the "Special Sales Department" at the address above.

KEEN/KARL D. KEEN
Hardback: 978-1-961123-19-9
Paperback: 978-1-961123-30-4
eBook: 978-1-961123-31-1

Contents

Dialogue

On October 29th nineteen and twenty-nine, which is now known as Black Tuesday, over sixteen million shares of stock were sold on the New York stock market, the value of stock fell rapidly leaving people in financial ruin. People made a run on the banks, trying to save what few dollars they had invested. Not having the currency on hand to pay off all the depositors the banks closed their doors, many to never open again. This caused a real panic in the nation and quickly spread around the world. The value of the dollar fell rapidly, to make matters worse foreign countries put an import tax on all goods bought and sold.

At the same time the dust bowl had hit the Midwestern states, leaving the farmers broke with no way to pay off their loans, many just moved off the land and never looked back.

During the fall of 1931 the international gold standard fell, completely removing any hope for recovery.

On November the first of that year the Carthage Grey Marble Company in Phenix, Missouri closed down. Leaving many families destitute. This is the story of the Keen family, how they suffered, fought and struggled to survive those bitter years. Men were jailed and families torn apart by crooked politicians, supported by crooked cops, all to gain power and finances at the expense of the poor. Strong men cried and weak men died as they fought to feed their families in a time that America should never forget.

These stories are true to the best of my memory and stories I have heard, some have been enhanced for reader enjoyment. Several of the names have been changed to protect those still living. I am 82 years old and I am writing things from memory, so anyone in the family that wants to correct or write their own indenture, feel free to do so. I am mostly writing this for my own family, but I sincerely hope others will add to it, as there is a lot of history in our family, the original name is KEEN, but it has been changed to KEENE, or KEANE, by some quirks of spelling. It doesn't matter as we are all family, and I love each and every one of you. I hope you enjoy what I have written.

Karl David Keen

Chapter One

The first effects of the panic in 1929 came to our home when my Granddad Harve Keen and our neighbor Mr. Willard lost their jobs at the marble quarry. Grandfather came home early that day, set his lunch bucket down on the kitchen counter and just sort of collapsed onto a wooden chair. He looked at my grandmother with tears in his weathered eyes, and with a trembling voice, he told her he had just lost his job. Telling her that the quarry foreman had let everyone go that didn't have children. And that the rest would be out of work by the end of the month. Due to the collapse of the stock market, there was no longer any money available for the polishing companies to buy stone. Grandfather being unable to read or write never had any idea what the stock market was. All he knew was that the marble company was in financial trouble and that everyone depending on them was too. The Phenix Grey Marble Company employed most everyone in the community, at one time, there was over two hundred and fifty men employed. It was a town with two stores, gas pump, hotel, post office, school, meeting hall, with most all of the houses belonged to the company. The houses were painted different colors depending on the number of bed rooms. Red houses had only one bed room the blue ones had two while the yellow houses had three. Everyone was paid with a script that was only redeemable at one of the company stores. If you got caught spending money in another town, it was a sure way to lose your job. As the word went, they owned everything and everyone in the community. However, if you had a real financial emergency, you could fill out papers at the bank and exchange script for cash at a reduced rate.

The only people out of their reach were the farmers, but in order to sell their produce they had to deal with the company in one way or the other. It owned the railroad spur that served the town and the surrounding area. The electricity and water were supplied by them at a much higher rate. Most of the houses had hand-dug wells where the water could be drawn up by hand; it was a lot of work to water cattle this way. It was surface water so had to be boiled before you could drink it.

Most people raised chickens and a few hogs to supplement their income. We had a milk cow and Dad sold cream and eggs to the company store but never got paid for it, they just kept a running tab for groceries, etc. Sometimes he would sneak eggs, cream, or a pig-out, and sell them to someone for cash money; he had to be very careful not to be seen with the money, as there would be questions asked as to where he came by it. The local law seemed to be everywhere and always kept an eye out for the company. They would report anyone that might be spending or earning money someplace else.

The county was run by an elected judge, that everyone just called Judge Brown. He never seemed to have anyone opposing him at election time. His nephew Bill O'Grady was the law. He was a big man standing over six feet four inches tall and weighing over two hundred and seventy pounds. He kept his dark red hair plastered slick to his scalp with Fitch's hair oil; Dad said he must use a bottle of it a day as he reeked from the stuff. The collar of his shirt was always grease-stained and it even ran down the back of his shirt at times. Grady, as everyone called him, had a mean streak and liked to bully people, he had beaten several men almost to death in the name of the law. They were all related to the marble company owners in some way. I heard my father say many times, "Slavery never ended it, just changed colors and masters". Even the local Doctor and Preacher were on the company payroll. There was no privacy for anyone. Dad always said, they knew when you went to shit and what color it was.

We were probably the largest family employed by the quarry. My father and three of his brothers worked there, plus my grandfather and two of his brothers and several of their sons. Grandfather was the powder, or dynamite man for the company, he couldn't read but always knew how much powder to put in a hole. Of the twenty-seven children in the country school, eighteen were Keens and all but two of the others were related to them. One of the other students was Bonnie Parker of Bonnie and Clyde fame. I am sure some other famous people attended that school but at this time, Bonnie is the only one that comes to mind.

##############

My father came home from work that same evening totally worn out both physically and mentally. Sitting his lunch pail down on the porch rail, he gave his wife a hug and set down on the porch steps. Pulling her down beside him he placed his tired hand on her arm and said, "Grandpa got laid off today and the rest of us will be out of work by the end of the month. They are closing down the quarry, only a few of us will get to work for a couple of weeks to secure all the machines and do some cleanup work."

Carl was a large man, standing nearly six-foot tall and weighing around one hundred and ninety pounds, he had the square build of the Sac Indians of that area, he was born with a lazy eye that never seemed to develop, leaving him blind in his right eye, he had huge strong arms developed from hard work at the quarry breaking rock, and from being raised on a farm. Only going to the sixth grade, he had a remarkable amount of intelligence, and could read and do figures with the best of people. He had a beautiful tenor voice and was known around the region for his singing ability, and was called on to sing at church and many other festivities. His two brothers Gene and Sterlin played wind instruments in the community orchestra, even singing on the radio station KWTO out of Springfield. Two of his sisters Marie, and Ester along with Brother Joe played the violin. His wife Myrtle had been his childhood sweetheart, being raised on a farm less than a mile from him. They had three children with another on the way. They had no money in the bank, but did have over seventy dollars in credit coming from the company store, from the sale of cream, eggs and some meat he had supplied the store with when he butchered the hogs.

Leaving the oldest girl Vera to watch the two younger children he got up, took Myrtle by the hand and walked over to grandfather's house, which was only a short distance away. Not knowing what he would say to his father, but feeling it necessary to be with him at this time. They slowly walked along not talking but each of them was completely engrossed in their own thinking. Carl noticed the Polk weeds and other greens that were growing along the path. Thinking to himself he smiled, well hell they could always graze like an old cow if things got that rough. He hated canned greens but they would sustain life and keep the kids belly full.

Grandmother met them at the door when they came up the path; she gave each of them a big hug, told them to come in and set, and that she would make everyone a hot cup of sassafras tea to sooth their nerves. Dad couldn't help noticing the tears in her eyes. She had been a beautiful red-headed girl, one of the Brady families, now her red hair was streaked with gray, and her ever-present smile and laughter had left lines in her face adding to her beauty. She dearly loved grandfather and all her children, each Sunday she would cook a large meal and invite everyone over.

Grandfather looked up at Dad as he came in, taking a drag from his old corn cob pipe he said, "Son, it looks like we are in for some hard times." Dad tried to smile but only half managed a grin, and said, "We're Keens, we have survived a lot of things and we will survive this, even if we have to steal from some rich son-of-a-bitch," both men laughed, as Dad pulled up a chair and sat down.

Granddad said, "We will let the other boys, Joe, Sterlin, Gene and Wilburn think on this for a day or two and all talk about it come Sunday dinner. We have a lot of family living here in these hills; we should be able to pull through if we all stick together. Hell, we can eat rabbits and squirrels until we shoot them all out. The river is full of fish and we can trap fur this winter. Those damn old tough coons are eatable if you grind them up. Each of us still has a few hogs to butcher and canned food in the cellar; we can make it easy for a year or two. Could cut a few cords of wood but will have to trade it to someone, I bet there aren't twenty dollars in this whole town. We may all have to move back to the farm as the company will want rent for these houses and I doubt if they will take their own damn script."

He told Dad that if he had any credit coming at the store, he better go use it up before the bastards raise their prices or else close the doors. This got Carl to worry, he got up and took Myrtle by the hand and said, "Come on woman, we are going shopping." Walking over to the store he told them he wanted a hundred pounds of sugar, a hundred pounds of dried beans, and ten pounds of coffee. He also got three sacks of flour, even though he knew it would be full of weevils before they could use it. They bought new shoes and clothes for all the kids, plus new shoes for themselves. Dad had to make several trips back and forth to carry it all home. After the purchases he still had over forty dollars on the books.

Walking back over to Grandfather's he asked if there was anything they needed. Grandmother told him to buy fruit jars and all the canning lids they had. On Dad's second buying spree, the man running the store asked him why he was stocking up, Dad just looked at him and smiled. With his last few dollars of credit, he bought a J.C. Higgins twelve-gauge shotgun, and several boxes of shells, plus two dozen number two steel traps.

Hard times might be coming but Dad was going to be ready to meet them head on. "Little did he know what lay ahead?" Having the storekeeper credit him with three months' rent on the house, he made sure everything he owed was paid up, maybe by then things would improve and everyone would be back at work. As he walked home, he couldn't help but feel the gnawing emptiness in his stomach. If this went on, how would he pay for the new baby and keep food on the table?

The next morning, over thirty men were gathered around the old coal stove at the company store, their weathered faces were all solemn and frowned with worry. These men all had families to feed and they depended on the marble company for their very existence, most of them owed money to the store, and they had no idea of how they could pay it.

They lived in company houses with no way to pay their rent. Even the Foreman and supervisors hadn't had any warning of the closure; they too were dependent on the marble company. A majority of the men were related, they were brothers, fathers and sons, and cousins. Most of them had grown up around Bolivar, Ash Grove and Walnut Grove before moving to Phenix to work in the quarry. The Keens, Bradys, and Kirks were all first cousins. With the Daniels, Higgins, and Tucks all being second and third cousins.

Plus, a couple hundred more around the area that were all related through marriage.

The men stood and talked about jobs they might get. The only paper that came was a weekly paper and most of the families never got it. They would drop by the store for any news and everything they were hearing was bad. Stories were told of men committing suicide because of going bankrupt. Most of these men never lost anything in the bank closure, as they just lived from check to check and it was only redeemable in company script. There probably weren't twenty dollars among all of them.

Chapter Two

After carrying everything home, Carl went through the excitement with the kids over their new shoes and clothes. Everything seemed to fit, which eased his mind some. It seemed he never had enough money to buy them much. One thing they always had was plenty to eat, and never once did any of them go to bed hungry. Myrtle kept the children clean and taught them to be well-mannered. It seemed like she was always pregnant, they had been married just a little over eight years and she was expecting their fourth child. This isn't what she wanted out of marriage.

Before they were married, Carl was always taking her to dances or a picnic somewhere, and they sang at the old Keel Hall every Friday and Saturday night. There were pie suppers, fish fries, square dances, and ball games to go to. Now it seemed like all she ever got to do was change diapers and wash dirty clothes. She had dreams of shiny cars, fancy clothes and of seeing the world. This caused friction between the young couple, Carl was quick to anger and with each fight they had, Carl would leave the house and spend hours with his friends until he cooled off.

Being out of a job and underfoot seemed to add to the couple's troubles; Carl would set alone and stare into the darkness. They only had a little over eleven dollars, and didn't own a vehicle or anything else of value. All they had was kids and a few sticks of furniture. Constant worry about how he would care for his family caused him to be on edge and it didn't take long for a fight to start.

Myrtle would leave the children with him and go for long walks; Always ending up at her parent's house. She seemed to spend a lot of time talking to Carl's cousin Otis and his parents. Carl had a bitter dislike for Otis, and felt he was always hanging around for the wrong reasons. Otis had dated Myrtle before she and Carl were married, which didn't help matters any, and she seemed to still have a fondness for him. When she walked to her parent's house, she had to pass his place on the way. He would come out of the house and talk with her for long periods at a time.

Her parents lived on the river about a mile down the road, and many times when she would walk over there, she would be gone for hours, which added to Carl's fury. He loved his children but didn't seem to have the patience that was required to handle them. He would often take the three kids over to his mom's and go looking for Myrtle, the harder it was to find her the madder he would get. When he would find her, he would go into a violent cussing rage that was aimed at whoever was around. Many of the family was afraid of him when he became angry, his younger brother Joe seemed to be able to handle him best, even though the two did have several fights. Carl loved his younger brother and never tried to really hurt him.

After these angry outbursts Carl would be ashamed of himself and apologize to everyone, he just couldn't seem to control his anger. Myrtle loved Carl very much, but she was becoming afraid of him, even though he never harmed her physically. His constant accusations and angry fits were starting to wear on their marriage. She was having a lot of sickness with this pregnancy and didn't have the energy to do the things that Carl seemed to demand of her.

The company house they were living in was to be torn down and moved, so Carl moved his family to the company hotel. This gave them more room but there was a man living there that Myrtle now had to cook and clean for, to help pay the rent. The quarry had shut down, and with it went all the water and electricity to the homes. Dad got a night watchman job with the company and now was gone all night. He tried to sleep for days but with the kids and the old man moving about, sleep was almost impossible.

Myrtle was so big now that she was miserable and unable to do much, Carl had to heat wash water outside over an open fire in the tubs and do the laundry, and this had to be done most every day. At times he would go over to his parents and try to sleep, leaving Myrtle alone to deal with the three kids.

The watchman job did little more than pay the rent, the pay he got was still in company script and only redeemable at the one store left in town. The bank was closed and the store only carried stale items that hadn't been sold. It was now a real struggle to feed the kids; Dad had to cut wood every spare moment he had trying to keep the old hotel warm.

Most of the people had moved away now that the water and electricity were cut off. The marble company had sold a lot of the houses and they were being moved daily by large house-moving trucks. People would move away leaving home canned fruit and vegetables in the cellars. Dad would collect these canned goods and bring them home to feed the kids. One day Sheriff Grady caught him with several jars of canned fruit from one of the cellars, he told Dad that all that stuff left behind now belonged to the marble company, and told him to pour it out on the ground. Carl tried to explain to him that there were hungry people all over the country that could use these canned goods. He told him to just look around at some of the children, they're all hungry. It isn't just his kids but everyone around here. People are living on wild greens and berries; the only meat on their tables is from some squirrel or rabbit they killed. "You have to be out of your mind to make me pour this stuff out." Grady said, "If l let people have this stuff, then they won't buy from the company store. I am just protecting the company's interest." This angered my Dad so much that he grabbed Grady by the shirt and pushed him backward, saying, "You ignorant red-headed son of a bitch. You don't work for the company; you're an elected county official." He could see the fear in Grady's eyes as he held onto his shirt.

Grady pulled a blackjack from his back pocket and told Carl to tum him loose or he would hit him with it. "You hit me with that, you red-headed son-of-a-bitch you better make sure it puts me down or I will stomp your ass all over this town."

Luckily! Brother Joe showed up about then and separated the two men. Grady told Carl he was under arrest for theft. Picking up the two jars of fruit Carl smashed them on the ground, turning toward Grady, he gave him a shove and said, "Well there is your damn evidence. Pick it up. And arrest me, for I ain't pouring anything out that will feed my kids or my neighbors."

Grady's greasy hair was going in every direction, and his face was as read as his hair. Carl stood there with every muscle tense, his face showing the hate he had for the man, he had his right fist doubled up ready to strike. Joe kept telling him to calm down. Finally, Grady slicked his oily hair back with one hand and said, "Keen, one of these days you're going to push things too far."

Carl told him, "Grady I will make a bet. Someone will kill your stupid red-headed ass before the winter is over. A judge or no Judge."

Joe pulled his brother away and tried to talk to him, telling him that he would probably lose his watchman's job over this.

Carl said, "That he didn't give a damn. That he was tired of that Fitch's hair oil-smelling son of a bitch bullying people. He will push the wrong man one of these days, and some good man will go to prison for killing that worthless bastard."

Joe took his brother by the arm and said, "Come on, let's go over to Mom and have her fix us a cup of tea." Granddad was sitting by the stove smoking his pipe when the two men came in. Joe told his father about the whole ordeal, Granddad took his pipe from his mouth, tapped it on the stove and said, "You boys better steer clear of Grady, he is the Judge's nephew and they stick together pretty close. Hell, boys, he has stolen all the farms and money in this county. He owned the bank and stole every dollar in it, then foreclosed on every farmer around here. Now he has opened up an orphanage so he can take people's kids and have the state pay him for taking them. Carl, you will be on the wise side to just stay away from him."

He just sat there sipping his tea not saying a word. Most of the anger had left him and he finally smiled, turned to Joe and said, "If you hadn't showed up when you did, I was about to pop that big-mouthed bastard right in the kisser."

Grandmother came in and told the two men to be on the lookout for a good sassafras bush when they were out and about. That she needed a supply of roots dug and dried if they expected to have tea this winter.

Carl got up and set his cup on the table, telling everyone he better get home that Myrtle was about to pop any time, so he better stick close to home.

The night watchman's job was boring, all he did was walk around and look at a bunch of big white marble rocks. No one ever came up there; he would set and sleep most of the nights now, waking up enough to make his rounds. One evening, he ran out of tobacco and walked home to fetch more. He found Otis sitting on the porch talking to Myrtle, instantly he flew into a jealous rage, grabbed Otis and knocked him to the ground, and kicking him before he could get up, he accused them of having an affair even though Myrtle was about to give birth. Telling Otis that he would kill him if he ever caught him talking to Myrtle again.

Myrtle walked over to her parents and spent the night. Carl had to get his mother to stay with the kids while he went back to work.

After work he walked over to get Myrtle, apologizing to her, telling her that the ordeal with Grady and not being able to provide much for the family was wearing on him.

Myrtle was so big now there was little she could do. Vera, the oldest girl, was almost nine and she and her younger sister, Jo Anna who was seven, helped a lot by doing most of the cooking under the watchful eye of their mother. They also had to care for their four-year-old brother, Harve, who was always into everything.

Myrtle soon gave birth to another boy, whom they named Muriel Don. She was very weak after the birth and her mother Mrs. Grant came over and helped the family. The old man had moved from the hotel so this lessened the burdensome. They no longer had to do his laundry and cooking and they now had the whole hotel to themselves. There were eight bedrooms, plus the kitchen, lobby, and dining room. Most of the rooms were kept closed off to keep from heating them. The empty rooms made a good place for the kids to play inside when the weather was bad.

Grady had gotten word of the fight between Carl and Otis, so he came down to talk to him about it. Carl told him it wasn't any of his damn business, and to get the hell away from him before he got his redheaded ass kicked. Reluctantly, Grady backed off telling Carl that he was headed for trouble. Everyone knew a fight was coming between the two men; it was just a matter of where and when.

Winter was coming on and Carl, Joe, and Granddad spent all of their spare time cutting wood. They hauled most of it in Granddad's wagon with the team of horses he kept. Carl and Joe set traps along Phenix Creek, Clear Creek, and all of the small farm pounds and drainage ditches that ran through all of the low places. They would get up early and run the traps, catching raccoon, muskrat, and an occasional mink. There was a lot of opossums in the area, and they sold them without skinning to a man over by Ash Grove who made dog food from them. This brought in a small amount of income, and with the rabbits and squirrels, they killed while out trapping helped feed the families.

The meat from the raccoons was ground up and mixed with rabbit meat and made into a sausage that was spiced with sage. When they butchered most all of the hog was used, they took the intestines and turned them inside out cleaned them good and used them to stuff the sausage into. All of the fat was saved and rendered into lard. The skin was cooked down and made into cracklings. The grease from the skin was mixed with lye, wood ashes, and some lilac root. This was cooked down and made into soap that was used for washing clothes and cleaning the tongue of some foul-mouthed boys.

Even the feet were cleaned, pickled and canned. As Dad used to say he would even use the squeal to make a whistle if he could catch it. The blood was caught and made into a blood pudding.

Granddad would catch skunks and skin them; he would render the grease out of their fat and make skunk oil. This he used to waterproof his boots and to oil things. He would even give a spoon full of it to a sick child; you got well quick as you sure didn't want the second dose.

He would gather green cockle burrs and boil them down into a syrup that he mixed with honey and whisky to make a good cough syrup. I can't remember how it tasted, but it had to be bad, as I don't remember any of his old remedies tasting good. The sassafras tea they made had a root beer taste that with a little honey was good, and it seemed to calm the nerves. They wouldn't let the kids drink much, but the adults drink a lot of it instead of coffee. I wish I remembered some of the old remedies, like the flax seed polis for boils; they used tobacco mixed with water to spray the garden plants and the inside of the chicken coop for mites. Coal oil was used on cuts and to prevent infection, sometimes it was even taken internally, for what I don't remember. The soot from the fireplace was kept and used to stop bleeding, the only thing was when it was applied to a cut it would leave a black tattoo of the cut that stayed on you forever. To cure an earache, a pipe was lit and the stem placed into the ear, then the smoke was blown backward through the pipe into the ear. A lot of people grew up back then and never saw a Doctor, as there were no phones and no way to get to a doctor in a hurry, so most ailments were treated at home.

People pulled teeth for each other and sewed up many a cut with a needle and a boiled thread. All children were born at home, no one ever heard of a woman going to a hospital to have a baby.

As things got tougher around Phenix, a lot of the young men would hop a freight train and ride to Kansas or Oklahoma, and work in the wheat harvest. Most every speck of land had been plowed up and put into wheat.

During the summer of 1931 no rain came and most of the wheat was short with not much grain on it. Many of the farmers plowed it under and tried to reseed it. As the drought continued the plowed fields got dryer and dryer, and the wind began to blow the soil from the tops of the fields. By now the cattle had severely overgrazed the pasture lands and it too begin to blow away. Winter came and with it no moisture, just a cold dry wind that froze everything around, ponds and streams began to dry up along with most of the shallow dug wells.

People were hauling water long distances trying to keep their cattle watered. Farmers were leaving their farms and moving west to California hoping to make a living in the fruit orchards. Soon great billowing clouds of dust were blowing across the landscape blocking out the sun.

President Hoover had tried everything to lessen the loss to the plain's farmers; nothing seemed to work, as the wind continued to blow away the topsoil. In 1932 there were a total of thirty-eight severe dust storms. Children were made to wear masks to keep from breathing the dirt into their lungs. Even the tightest build houses were filled with the powder. It would blow in through keyholes and around windows and doors. Some storms would make the day as dark as night. These storms became known as Black blizzards.

Cattle were forced into fence corners where they died of suffocation and were soon buried by the ever-drifting and blowing clouds of dust. Franklin Roosevelt was elected president under the guise of a new recovery act.

One of the first things he did was to declare a four-day bank holiday, after which he got Congress to enact the Emergency Banking Act, this stabilized the banking industry and restored people's faith in the banking system by putting the federal government behind it.

More and more of the Keen family that had drifted into Kansas and the great plains were returning to the hills seeking a way to feed their families. Many had nothing but a beat-up old car and clothes on their backs. The children were hallowed-eyed and very thin. All of them looked like war refugees, but the family took care of the family and soon they were located someplace and all got fed. Many of them regrouped and moved their families to California, where they were turned back at the border by the Los Angeles police, who had been sent there by their chief to keep them out of the area.

As more of them moved into the San Joaquin, Valley of California, Shanty towns began to grow as shacks made from tin and cardboard or anything else they could find to live under began to pop up along the fields. Due to the poor living and working conditions, a Union was formed by the Cannery and Agriculture workers, a strike was called and rioting broke out among the workers. The strike lasted for twenty-four days with the death of three people and hundreds being severely beaten by thugs hired to make them work.

Word soon found its way back to Phenix that everything in California wasn't as good as people had expected it to be. Carl gave up all idea of moving his family west.

Chapter Three

A lot of the families had moved, and the little country school of Phenix had dwindled down from twenty-seven students to sixteen. Eleven of the remaining kids were from the Keen families. They were brother and sister and first and second cousins. The teacher was a Mrs. Daniels and she also was a distant cousin. Most everyone in that area was related to the Keen family in one way or the other. They stuck together and helped one another through the hard times as best they could.

Our neighbor Mr. Arthur was the secretary and treasurer of the little school district. He always kept the school money in a little cigar box, until such time he could get to Ash Grove, where the new bank was now located. Art, as everyone called him, had a nice farm located along the banks of Clear Creek, he worked hard farming the land and caring for his cattle. His wife Edna had born him nine children that he was very proud of. Mr. Arthur had lost almost everything when the depression hit. The local bank had closed and taken every penny he had saved in it. Judge Brown was trying to foreclose on their farm; he had taken Art's money when the bank closed, and now he was trying to take the land under the name of a bank that no longer existed. He had opened up another bank, under government approval, only this time they had to insure each customer's account. People were now afraid of the banks and no one in Phenix had two cents to put in one anyway. Why Mr. Arthur trusted one again was a question to everyone around.

Mr. Arthur's brother that lived in California was sending him money to pay for a lawyer, this angered Judge Brown, and his nephew Grady didn't miss any opportunities to tell everyone about it. He would bully Mr. Arthur every chance he got, even giving him a traffic ticket for some trumped-up reason, he would accuse him of everything that happened. The Judge owned two adjoining farms and wanted the Arthur place that lay between them and the river. Art wouldn't sell, and with the help of his brother, was managing to squeeze out a living on the farm and pay the mortgage each year.

Judge Brown kept raising his taxes and interest on the mortgage. Most people trusted the banker and had signed floating mortgage rates when they borrowed money from the bank. The Judge had full control of the county and with the law being on his side managed to steal several farms that the bank had loaned money on. He now was raising property taxes so that most people couldn't pay them.

Grady was the tax collector, he took people's furniture, automobiles, farm machinery, and anything they had of value, in order to collect the tax money owed. It wasn't long until every cellar was stripped of canned food. Every scrap of metal had been sold and any wild berries or editable plants had been stripped from the land. Proud people were begging for work, or food for their children.

Mr. Arthur had bought two sacks of feed for his cattle; cashing a warrant that was made out to the school and used three dollars of the money to pay for the feed. He put the change into his pocket and drove to the bank, where he withdrew three dollars from his account, and deposited it along with the rest of the money in the cigar box into the school's account.

The feed store worker told Grady that Mr. Arthur had taken money from the school's warrant and paid for the feed with it.

Grady run to the judge with this information and had a warrant written up for the arrest of Mr. Arthur for using school funds for his own personal use. That afternoon he drove out to Arthur's farm and arrested Mr. Arthur in front of his family, putting handcuffs on him. Saying was under arrest for stealing school money, and that he was going to jail. Mrs. Arthur told one of the boys, to run to Harve Keen's for help, Granddad sent him over to Carl's and to some of the other boy's houses. When they got there Grady had already gotten the car out to the main road. Dad, Granddad, Joe and Lawrence Brady our cousin stood in the middle of the road to stop the car.

Grady swung the car over into the ditch, gunned the motor and drove past everyone, none of the men had a car so couldn't give chase. Soon about forty men, some with guns were heading for town on foot in wagons and in a few cars. Word of Mr. Arthur's arrest spread like wildfire through the hills of southern Missouri, it wasn't long until the little town of Ash Grove was full of angry men, some of them armed.

By now Grady and the Judge were both hated men, they had bankrupt, cheated, and foreclosed on most of the people in the county. A lot of these men had nothing left to lose, they knew they would eat better in jail than they were eating now. Judge Brown had turned one of the large farms into an orphanage; he had taken a lot of the children away from these people that couldn't feed them. The state was paying him so much per child to run the orphanage, and he put the bigger kids to work on one of the many farms he had. It was nothing short of slave labor, and the government was paying him to use them. The crowd kept growing and getting louder.

The state police finally showed up and were trying to disperse the crowd, Judge Brown stood in front of the jail trying to explain to the crowd that he and Grady were only doing their jobs. Each time he would try to speak he would be shouted down. Someone in the crowd shot a gun, the police and the judge all run for cover while the rest of the crowd hooted and laughed. Each time the judge would try to speak another shot would ring out, the three state police officers were trying to calm everyone and they weren't having much luck doing it. Grady was scared stiff, and his red face was as white as ash.

Finally, Mr. Arthur was brought out and the judge said that he was releasing him on fifty dollars bail and that he was going the bail for him. That a trial date had been set, and notice of the date would soon be posted. Art, as everyone called him, walked out into the crowd shaking hands with my grandfather and everyone else. Someone had brought Mrs. Arthur to town, she ran to Art, crying, and hugging him, asking him what this was all about.

Art set down on a step in front of the jail and told everyone he had come to town to buy some feed. That he stopped at the feed store first before going to the bank. And that he cashed a warrant that was made out to the school and used three dollars to pay for the feed.

Afterward he went to the bank, took three dollars of his money and replaced it in the cigar box, then deposited all of the school's money in the bank. That Burt down at the feed store saw him do it and sent Grady to him for using the school's money. He said he didn't feel like he had done anything wrong, and for everyone to go on home before we all get into trouble.

Turning toward Mrs. Arthur, he said, "I used some bad judgment, I guess. I should have gone to the bank first, but it was clear on the other end of town. Hell, I wasn't trying to steal the school's money. But I can see now how it must have looked to Burt. I have known him for twenty years; we have hunted and fished together. This damn depression has gotten everyone scared of their shadows, and the law is just standing around like a pack of damn vultures waiting for someone to steal an apple, so they can put them to work on one of the judge's farms."

Most everyone had gone on about their business by now, Art and his wife got up, walked over to my grandfather and said, "Come on Harvey, I will buy you a cold root beer." The three of them walked down to the filling station where they kept a wooden barrel full of bottled iced down root beer. Art found his wife an old chair to set in, while the two men stood there drinking the cold liquid.

Granddad asked Art what he thought the judge would do to him. Art just shrugged his shoulders and said, "That was sure a damn stupid thing to do. He will probably hit me with a big fine of some kind. Hell, I might have to spend a week in jail. Who knows what that power-hungry son of a bitch will do to a man? I know he wants my farm awfully bad. If it wasn't for the help from my brother Bill in California, he would already have it."

Art's car was still at his farm and it was a three mile walk back to Phenix, so the three of them started out on their trek home. It was a walk that my grandfather made every Saturday morning so he knew the road well. They would stop at each stream and watch the water for a while before walking on. Granddad could tell by the expression on Mr. Arthur's face that he was very worried about what had happened. He himself wondered what they would do to him. He didn't see anything wrong with what Art did. But the law had a different way of looking at things.

They seemed to write laws to favor the rich and powerful. These were hard times and the law ruled as it wished. Well, those enforcing it did. Granddad could feel the tension in the air and knew that things would get bloody before this damn depression was ever over. He figured it would come to another civil war, the poor and starving folks against the rich and powerful. Anyway, if it happened, America would lose. He wondered what was going on in the rest of the world. He had never been to a big city but had heard stories of them. and saw a few pictures of all the tall buildings, with cars going in every direction; he sure didn't want anything to do with any big city. He would be happy to just live and die here in these hills.

After they got home Granddad told Grandma about what had happened, and that they had set a trial date for Art. He and Mr. Arthur had been friends since they were young boys; both of them starting school together. Granddad had dropped out of school after the first grade and worked on the farm. Art had gone on through school and even attended a couple of years of high school. All Granddad knew was that his friend was in trouble and he didn't have any money or any way to help him.

Chapter Four

The whole community was upset over Mr. Arthur being arrested. Some people felt he did wrong, but others didn't see any wrong in it. Most did think he used bad judgment in his decision to pay for the feed with school money, but no one could see any attempt on his part to steal from the school. It was just a bad decision that snowballed. Now Art was in serious trouble with the law. If that damn Burt would have just kept his big mouth shut no one would have known about it.

A date was set for the trial, and the judge had paid the bail for Mr. Arthur, most folks felt he only did this to try and cover the fact that he was after Art, and his farm. No one had any money to help hire a lawyer, and they didn't trust them anyway, but Art sure needed help. There was a meeting held at the Keel Hall, with close to a hundred people showing up, there were cars, horses, and wagons, and buggies parked everywhere. Some of these people hadn't been out of the hills for over a year.

A lot of good things were said about Mr. Arthur and a lot of bad things were said about the judge and Grady. There was talk about just killing the no-good bastards, tar and feathering them and riding them out of town on a rail.

Mr. Smith stood up and said, "This is a Klan matter and we will meet at my barn tomorrow night." Everyone agreed and the meeting ended with a big potluck dinner following it. Groups of men and women stood around eating and discussing what was to take place.

Mr. Arthur walked around from group to group shaking hands and thanking people; he finally stood on a chair and apologized to everyone for what he did. Saying he had just used poor judgment. That he had no intention of stealing the school funds, that it was just quicker and easier to stop at the feed store first, and then go on to the bank.

Several men wanted to go get Burt and run him out of the country, Burt had a lot of kin at the meeting, who stood up and disowned him for being on the judge's payroll. There were a million words spoken but nothing said that could help Art.

The Klan met the next evening in Mr. Smith's barn, it was so crowded with men and boys that most had to stand outside and try to hear what was being said. They decided to get as many Klan members as possible on the jury, that way they could find Art innocent. Everyone agreed to let the law take its course, surely some of the Klan members would be picked for the jury.

When the date for the trial came around, the Judge moved the trial to Springfield, where Mr. Arthur wasn't known and none of the local people could get on the jury. This really sent a storm wave through the hills. Springfield was twenty miles away, and to some of the hill people it might as well have been a hundred. They just couldn't leave their farms and animals alone that long, as it was too far to go by wagon or horseback. Those that still owned cars didn't have any money for gasoline.

Grandfather said he was going if he had to walk there and sleep on the courthouse lawn. He wasn't going to stand by and see his friend railroaded by a crooked judge and that damn greasy-haired cop Grady.

On the morning of the trial, Grady drove out and again handcuffed Mr. Arthur in front of his family and pushed him into the police car. Granddad, Carl, Joe and Mr. Brady drove behind them in Mr. Brady's car. Followed by several other vehicles, that unknown to them were unmarked state police cars.

At the courthouse, there was a crowd of strangers that yelled and hollered at the cops as they took Mr. Arthur inside. Granddad smiled at Dad and said, "Looks like the Klan got the word out. Hell, we might just get old Art set free yet."

As the trial started Burt was the first witness called. He told how Mr. Arthur came in and ordered two sacks of seed grain, when he told him how much it was, he took a warrant that was made out to the school, from the school money box and used it to pay for the feed, and he gave Art back sixty-three cents in change, which Mr. Arthur put into his own pocket, not back in the box with the rest of the school's money. That he didn't see Art go to the bank, and he thought that being as Mr. Arthur paid for the feed with school money, he figured he better tells the law. Mr. Arthur's lawyer protested and asked Burt how he knew it was school money that Art used to pay for the feed.

Burt said, "Everyone knows Art keeps the school's money in that cigar box. And the warrant was made out to the

Phenix school district." The defense lawyer asked Burt if Art could have had some of his own money in that box.

Burt scratched his head and said, "Well it's possible I guess," but it sure looked like school money to him. The lawyer asked him how much different school money looked from regular money. This brought a laugh from the audience. The judge rapped his gavel and called for order.

After the defense lawyer was finished with Burt, Mr. Arthur was called to the stand.

He was sworn in and asked to tell the truth. Art admitted to cashing a three-dollar warrant out of the cigar box, but not to have any intentions of stealing it, as he had money in the bank to replace it with, and was headed to the bank next to deposit the school's money. He said, he withdrew three dollars from his account at the bank put it in with the school funds and deposited them in the school's account.

He stated that some people might see it as wrong doing but he couldn't see where he had done anything wrong.

The prosecutor asked him why he put the change in his own pocket instead of back in the box if he wasn't intending to steal it.

Mr. Arthur said, "It was just easier to keep track of three dollars than worry about the change."

The attorney asked Art how many times before he had used school money for his own personal use. Mr. Arthur said, "That he didn't ever recall using any of it before." The prosecutor waved his arms in the air and said, "All these years you have been trusted with the school's money, and now you will have us to believe that only on this one occasion you chose to spend it on yourself."

Art said, "I know it was a fool thing to do but I was just trying to save some time. I knew I had money in the bank to cover it and I would be replacing it in just a few short minutes. Sometimes I keep the money for over a week before I get to the bank to deposit it."

The prosecutor asked why he just didn't wait a week to replace the three dollars and draw interest on the school's money. Art looked like a beaten man, bowing his head he said, "I can see how this looks to some people, but I wasn't stealing it."

"Well, Mr. Arthur what do you call it?" He was asked. Before Art could answer the attorney said, "You buy grain with the school's money and just because you put it back, you want us to believe you weren't stealing it. If Burt Olson hadn't seen you taking the money, it most likely would still not have been replaced as you keep the books and no one sees them but once a year. You could wait for the next audit to replace the money, isn't that true?"

Art said in almost a whisper, "I have never in all my life ever taken something that wasn't mine. I have worked hard all my life, supporting the church and school. I have served my country through the war, been wounded twice, was honorably discharged and have been a law-abiding citizen all my life. I am not a thief."

With this said, the court took a brief recess, and Arthur was again moved from the court room in handcuffs. Edna, his wife, just sat there and cried along with Art's two oldest boys.

When the court reconvened, Judge Brown asked if anyone else had any evidence pertaining to these matters. The courtroom was so quiet you could hear Art take a deep breath and exhale it.

The Judge rapped his gavel on the bench and said, "Andrew Arthur buy your own admittance in taking school funds and using them to pay a personal bill, I have no alternative but to find you guilty as charged.

"This is a very serious crime; you were trusted to handle the public's money but you betrayed that trust for your own personal gain. These are hard times and people work hard to pay their taxes, it is a daily struggle for most Americans to feed their families. They have to be able to trust their public officials," (this brought a loud laugh from the courtroom). The judge again rapped the gavel and called for order, reminding everyone that he would clear the courtroom with the next outburst.

He asked Mr. Arthur to stand for sentencing, telling him that it was the court's responsibility to watch over public trust and to punish those that betray it. "And Andrew Arthur by your own admission of guilt, I have no choice but to sentence you to five years hard labor in the Missouri state prison. This sentence is to start immediately."

The courtroom interrupted in and out roar as the state police officers again handcuffed Arthur and led him from the courtroom, not even letting him say goodbye to his family. Judge Brown along with Constable O'Grady slipped quietly out of sight into a back room before anyone had time to notice.

My grandfather stood there on the courthouse steps with tears streaming down his brown weathered cheeks, saying I have just seen the biggest misuse of justice that I have ever heard of. Dad took him by the arm and led him over to Brady's car, saying someone will kill those two worthless bastards before this is over.

Granddad pulled loose and went back into the courthouse, where he talked to Art's wife, telling her that he and the boys would help her and the kids work the farm. She stood there shaking and told him everything was lost, that Art had borrowed all he could on the farm to pay for the lawyer, that they didn't have enough money left to pay the taxes on it.

Art's son Bob said, "That damn judge may get the farm, but I will burn ever damn building on it down if he does, along with everything he owns, Hell maybe they will put me in a cell with my father."

A large crowd had gathered out front, waiting for the judge and Grady to come out, but they had already slipped out a back door and were safely gone.

The ride back to Phenix was a quiet sober trip, no one spoke much. Granddad just sat there holding his pipe, a sad expression on his face, finally, he spoke saying, "I wonder which of us will be the next one they come after."

He didn't know it then, but within a few short weeks, one of his sons would be arrested and put in jail for suspicion of murder?

More and more people were moving to the west coast or at least trying too. Roosevelt signed the Farm Mortgage Act that allotted 200 million dollars to help farmers that were losing their farms due to foreclosure, this set up a local bank and credit association. The Judge jumped right on this deal and tried to get control of the local office.

People were still going hungry; there just wasn't any money in circulation. If people had any money, they were afraid to spend it. Prices of hogs and cattle had hit rock bottom. Certain counties were classified as Drought Relief Counties and cattle were bought by the government for as little as fourteen dollars a head. Over six million head of hogs and cattle were destroyed by the government to try and bring up prices.

This brought such a public outcry from the starving population that a quick government program was started, called the Federal Surplus Relief Corporation. This program diverted agriculture commodities to relief organizations. Apples, beans, canned beef, flour and pork products were distributed through local relief channels. Cotton goods were eventually included to clothe the needy and to keep the big cotton growers on the side of the government. Mr. Roosevelt had the population right where he wanted them, everyone was now depending on the government and they were afraid to vote him from office.

As the dust storms continued, over a hundred million acres of formerly cultivated land had been destroyed as for raising crops. President Roosevelt signed the Taylor Grazing Act, which allowed a hundred and forty million acres of federal land to be established into grazing districts. This helped arrest the deterioration, but couldn't undo the damage; it just added more government involvement as part of the New Deal.

Other government programs like the Shelterbelt Project, which encouraged and paid people to plant trees along fence rows and road ways, this program alone cost over seventy-five million dollars and added to the ever-growing government. Roosevelt was soon to change this program to the Work Project Administration, which would employ hundreds of thousands of men across the nation.

Chapter Five

It took several weeks for the little community of Phenix to settle down and realize that a beloved friend was now in prison for a petty mistake. No one could make themselves believe that Mr. Arthur had gotten five years for using less than three dollars of the school's money.

Granddad was so upset all he could do was chop wood, pretending each swing of the axe was coming down on the Judge's neck. Grady kept a low profile for a few weeks, arriving at the Arthur farm one morning to serve eviction papers on Mrs. Arthur.

Grady had papers to send five of the children to the judge's orphanage. He wanted the older boys to go to one of the judge's farms for orphaned boys, but they refused, telling him he could go to hell. That they were going to their uncles in California.

Grandfather tried to help Edna keep the kids, but the judge had seen to it that she had no money left to feed them with, as the court had left her without anything. Mr. Brady drove her along with what few possessions she had left to her sisters in Springfield. Grady had taken most of their machinery and furniture to pay the taxes. And the judge was trying to foreclose on the note that Art had signed with the bank that failed. Mrs. Arthur, asked if there was no longer a bank, how could they foreclose?

The Judge was the ruler of the county and no one seemed to want to question him. He was a duly elected county official, and his word was law. He had O'Grady and his deputies to back up his decisions. People lived in fear of them; they would sentence men to two years of labor working on one of the farms for no more than being drunk.

Mrs. Arthur had given my granddad a milk cow and three hogs, telling him to pay for them whenever he could. That she would rather he took them, than for the Judge to get his hands on them.

Carl lost his night watchman job, over the shoving match he had with Grady, which added more hate to the already boiling pot. He walked the country side over and back trying to find any kind of job he could.

He got a job helping the house movers jack up the houses; all nine of the homes along Brady's row were now being moved. Most of all Grandma's people had left for California, leaving only a few of the Brady clan scattered among the hills. This job did little more than pay the rent; everything had been moved out of the quarry leaving huge piles of rock and an old spar pole that was used to drag the huge blocks up out of the holes.

Our cousin Mr. Kirk gave Dad a job milking cows, for twenty-five cents a week and a gallon of fresh milk each day. He had to get up at four in the morning and walk two miles and then walked back over at four in the afternoon, some nights he didn't get home until after dark. Carl didn't like Mr. Kirk; says he was the tightest son of a bitch he had ever seen. That he would squeeze a nickel until the buffalo shit.

Just before Thanksgiving, Carl got up to go milk. Myrtle wasn't in the bed, he guessed she had gone to the outhouse so he waited as long as he could for her to return, then went out looking for her. He searched the place over, wakening up Vera to help look for her mother.

Having no idea where Myrtle might have gone, he left Vera there with the kids and walked over to her folks, she wasn't there and her Mom acted strange but swore she had no idea where she might have gone. Carl asked her to go stay with the kids until he could get back from work.

Plowing himself into the task at hand, he milked the cows as fast as he could and almost ran home. There still wasn't any sign of Myrtle. Dad walked over to Granddad's and told them Myrtle was missing. Granddad walked over to his Brother Charlie's place and asked if Otis had been around, Uncle Charlie hadn't seen or heard from Otis in several months.

Grandma walked over to Carl's to help Mrs. Grant with the kids, Carl was now in a near panic, soon panic turned to anger and he started cussing Myrtle and everyone she knew. He walked up thorough the quarry and searched all the deep pools where the rocks had been mined.

Going back to work and again milking as fast as he could, he left the barn dirty, walked over to the clear creek and walked its banks clear up to Phenix creek, then walked the creek back up past town. It was dark by the time he got home; tears filled his eyes as he started to realize that maybe Myrtle had left him. He knew she was very unhappy with having all the kids, and the last one had really left her in a deep depression. He was angry at himself, it seemed like all he had to do was take off his pants and she would be pregnant again.

Grandma and Mrs. Grant went home leaving him there with four small children. Vera fixed dinner, with the help of Jo Anna, they felt sad for their Dad and were very worried about their mother being gone. Carl set up most of the night just staring into the darkness, he loved Myrtle with all his heart, but he could see where he hadn't been the best husband, he just couldn't seem to control his temper. He finally fell asleep there in the chair, wakening up at about five a.m., he woke Vera and told her to watch the kids as he had to go to work. The barn and cows were a mess; he hadn't cleaned anything in two days so it took him all day to clean the barn, the milking equipment, and tend to the cows. It was nearly dark when he got back home.

The baby Don was very sick and running a fever, he wouldn't stop crying and little Vera had done everything she knew how to help her baby brother. Carl bundled him up and carried him over to his mother's, she said they would keep him there and care for him.

Carl was exhausted, and the house was a mess, plus all the clothes needed washing along with most of the baby's diapers. Building a large fire outside he heated tubs of water and washed all the clothes on a wash board. The smell of the diapers gagged him, no wonder the boy was sick, if what was coming out of him smelled like that. It took him until after midnight to finish the wash.

The alarm went off way too early, he hated to wake Vera up again this early. Standing by her bed he watched the little girl in her deep sleep, tears ran down his cheeks as he shook her awake. This was too much of a burden to put on a little nine-year-old girl.

Grandma kept Don and Harve while she and Joanna went to school. Most of the day was spent at Carl's house cleaning and fixing a hot meal for him and the girls.

Word spread quickly through the hills and soon all of the families were out looking for Myrtle. She had just completely vanished, leaving behind most of her clothes and the four children.

Carl was busy milking on the third day after Myrtle had disappeared, hearing a noise he looked up, he saw Grady with his deputy Clarence our cousin and another deputy named Bob standing and looking down at him. Grady told Carl to stand up and turn around, to put his hands behind his back that he was under arrest, not telling him why. This was the last straw; Carl came up with the milk stool and threw it at Grady's head knocking him back against the wall. In the same motion, he hit Cousin Clarence in the face knocking him down between two cows that started kicking and stepping on him. The other Deputy ran from the barn and came back with a shotgun. By that time Grady had gotten to his feet and tackled Carl sending both men into the stanchions that held the cows. As Carl fell backward, he reached over and flipped the lever open that held the cows, turning them all loose, now there were cows and men tangled in one big fight. Carl kept hitting.

Grady as the big man head-butted him, and the greasy oil from his hair was now getting into his eyes, as Grady kept butting him with his head.

Clarence had finally gotten to his feet only to be knocked backward by Carl again, this time he ran toward the front of the barn, where he met Bob with the shotgun. Grady was still trying to wrestle Carl to the ground, he was much bigger than him, but he didn't have the hard muscle that Carl possessed, and he was like a crazed animal. For the first time in a fight, Grady was scared, he knew Carl hated him enough to kill him and he wasn't getting any help from his Deputies.

Drawing the blackjack from his pocket he struck Carl on the side of the head knocking him down, but before he could strike again a cow stepped between the two men giving Carl time to get to his feet, this time he came up with a milk stool and swung at Grady, Bob had gotten into the barn by now, and shoved the shotgun into Carl's back telling him to freeze. Carl slapped the gun aside and walked from the barn. Turning toward Grady he said, "You better have that son of a bitch kill me right now for this ain't over."

Looking at Cousin Clarence he said, "How could you side with this low-down bunch of bastards, don't you have any family pride? My Dad always said you were a worthless son of a bitch, and that you had to come from someone else's loins, there was no way you could be a Keen."

Clarence just stood there looking at him. "Carl," he said "If it wasn't for the fact that I am here, these men would have already shot you, and me helping take you to jail will keep you from getting the hell kicked out of you once you are behind bars.

"I don't really give a damn what the rest of the Keen family thinks of me, I have never cheated or mistreated any of them, and I won't start now."

Grady stood there puffing with the sweat mixed with the Fitch's hair oil running down his red face. There was a large blue bruise on the side of his head where the milk stool had connected. Carl had a large bump on the side of his cheek where Grady had hit him with the blackjack. He rubbed his cheek, and said, "You would never have hit me if l could see out of that eye, I have been blind in it since birth." Bob was still standing there pointing the shotgun at Carl. Clarence walked over and told him to put up that damn gun before someone got killed. At the same time taking Carl by the arm, he apologized and said, "Carl, I have to put these on you. I will put them in front if you will promise to behave, and I will ride along to jail, and make sure nothing happens to you. They believe you have killed Myrtle and hidden her body."

Carl asked if he could go get someone to take care of the kids. Clarence told him that the county orphanage was already over there picking up the kids. It was a good thing they had handcuffs on Carl, for he went into another rage cussing the judge and everyone around. He said, "Granddad and the rest of the family will never let you bastards take those kids. One of you son of a bitches will get killed before this is over. I haven't harmed that damn woman; I don't even know where she is. You bastards have pushed people about as far as they will stand for it."

Grady gave off with a sigh and told Clarence to put him in the car. Clarence said they had better take Carl to Springfield as he had relations all over Ash Grove and as soon as the word got out there would be armed men all over the country looking for them.

He told Grady, "You better hope he is guilty and that you can prove it. I wouldn't want to be walking in your shoes, or even be in the county if we have to turn him loose. There are five of those boys and his father has four brothers, all with sons and grandsons in these hills, some of them spell the Keen name with an e on the end of it. But let me tell you they are all of the same blood, and they won't run from a fight. If you tangle with one you will have to whip them all. My mother was a Keen; there are so damn many cousins that you can't name them all. And there must be fifty or more of the Bradys around here. Hell Grady, your old lady might even be a Keen."

This didn't sit well with Grady, his head hurt where he had gotten hit by the milk stool, and Carl had landed some good punches on him. He thought about how tough and strong he had been. He wondered what had happened to Carl's wife, had he really killed her and hid the body or had she just run off? He knew that from his tangles with Carl that he must be hell to live with. He never knew about the blind eye that would account for some of his quick temper. Hell, he hadn't signed the arrest warrant, "the damn Judge had", all he was doing was what he was paid for. And by God today he wasn't paid enough. Now he would have to watch out for every damn Keen and their relatives in these hills.

They took Carl to Springfield and booked him into the Greene County jail for suspicion of murder. The county put the four children into one of the judge's orphanages, even taking the baby.

The next morning Grady and four men were seen dragging the quarry holes and the river. Another bunch of deputies went all over the county side looking for a newly dug grave. Granddad and Uncle Joe went with them. Neither of the men thought that Carl had harmed Myrtle but they couldn't tell these stupid bastards that, so they just tagged along. The Deputies dug around the two lime kilns, and any large rocks that looked like they had been moved. Stories spread around the little communities of Phenix, Ash

Grove, and Walnut Grove, where Carl's three younger brothers went to school. People stood in small groups talking among themselves making sure there was no Keen relation around to hear their warped stories.

Bloodhounds were brought in, to search the woods. Hay stacks were probed, and garden plots were dug up. Every place where any dirt had been disturbed was checked and rechecked. Weeks dragged by with nothing being found.

###############

Each day Carl was assigned to the county road crew, he was forced to work twelve hours a day cleaning ditches and filling potholes. The prisoners were required to wear blue shirts and pants with a white stripe along the leg. The shirt had a prisoner of Greene County stenciled across the back of the shirt. The men were shackled and chained on their trip to and from the work site, and made to wear leg chains all day long, which only allowed them to take small steps.

Carl fought back the dregs of depression, wondering where Myrtle was; surely, she wouldn't let him spend years in jail. What about a trial? He was arrested for suspicion of murder; when would they give him a hearing of some kind? He didn't have money for a lawyer. His mind kept going back to Mr. Arthur's trial, and how he got five years for spending less than three dollars of the school's money.

A month dragged by, and still no word of Myrtle. Granddad came to see him one Sunday morning bringing him a carton of cigarettes, and told him that the judge wouldn't let him see the kids so he could just guess that they were all right. Dad broke down and cried, telling his father that he hadn't harmed Myrtle, and that he had no idea where she might be. He said, "That damn Grady has been after my ass for years, and now it looks like he finally got it."

Granddad told him that Grady hadn't charged him with resisting arrest. That cousin Clarence had talked him out of it. He also said, "that you had put up one hell of a fight, and that Bob was about to shoot you when you quit. Hell son, you are lucky to still be alive. If you would have owned anything that damn Judge would have had you killed, just so he could get his hands on it.

"If they don't find Myrtle pretty quick, you will be plowing fields on one of the judge's farms for the next ten years, along with the rest of the people he and Grady have railroaded."

Days crept by, with Carl getting more and more depressed, he became withdrawn into himself spending his nights just lying awake and staring at the bottom of the bunk above him, sleep wouldn't come except in just short naps. The guards on the work crews were now pushing him trying to get him to work, he would set down and tell them, "Just shoot me you son of a bitches I haven't harmed anyone, but if l can get my hands on a gun, I will kill every bastard that looks at me." They couldn't get him to eat and he wouldn't drink anything, the guards were getting worried about him, he had lost probably forty pounds and the black circles around his eyes made him look years older than he was.

He had developed a sickening cough, but wouldn't quit smoking, the jail doctor took him off of the work crew for a week, and even this seemed to add to his anger. Along with the fact he hadn't been given a hearing date, or even talked to by anyone. It was like no one cared if he was innocent or not. They were just going to let him rot in jail.

Chapter Six

Another week went by and Carl's brother Joe showed up, and told him that Myrtle was in California, that she had written a letter to her sister in Oklahoma. They were trying to get the Judge to confirm it. He said he asked the judge to release him but he wouldn't until he could make sure the letter was from Myrtle, and that she was alive and well.

He said, "That it seemed damn funny they could put a man in jail just because they thought someone was missing, but they couldn't release you until their thoughts were proven wrong."

This perked Carl up some; he began to sleep at night and asked to go out with the road crew again. As he worked, he would sing a song about Grady that he had made up, it was how he was going to kick Grady's red ass, and run him from the hills with a pack of hounds for putting him in jail.

One of the guards told him he should quit singing it because the judge would never let him loose if he thought he was going after Grady. Another week went by with still no word of his release. Carl asked to talk to the Judge; he was taken into the Judge's offices Monday morning by two armed deputies. He asked the Judge to release him, and to give him back his children. The Judge told him he could be released on a thousand dollars bail; this angered Carl until he almost lost control. He stood there with his mouth open not saying a word. Finally, he asked the Judge where in the hell would he get a thousand dollars, when he didn't have a nickel to his name. The Judge asked him how he was going to feed his kids once he was released, as he was sure Mr. Kirk had hired someone else by now.

Carl told him he had canned goods and a couple of hogs he hadn't butchered, and that his folks would help him until he got on his feet. The judge told him he no longer lived at the hotel as he hadn't been able to pay rent while he was in jail, and that everything he owned had been impounded by the quarry to pay what he owed.

This hit Carl like a bullet, he stood there and asked the Judge where any justice had been served. "I never harmed anyone, and out of the blue that damn Grady and his deputies come to the farm where I was working, and without saying a word about why I was being arrested they put handcuffs on me. Hell, they wouldn't even wait while I finished milking.

"Now you tell me I have lost my job, been kicked out of my house, and everything I owned taken from me. You have taken my children and put them somewhere I don't even know. You have taken the food I had stored to feed them through the winter. Tell me again how justice is being served. Your honor this is why the prisons are so full of poor people, the government is pushing people to the breaking point.

"I will admit I have a violent temper, and I may not have been the best husband in the world. But my kids always had clean clothes to wear, a warm bed to sleep in, and a full belly. By God, I never once ever asked any son of a bitch for anything. But I am asking you now to turn me loose and give me back my kids; I will feed and shelter them somehow.

"These are hard times and hard times make for hard people. If you and Grady keep running roughshod over the people in these hills, a revolt is going to take place, and you sir, are the person with the most to lose. I am sure what you are doing is within the written law, but there is an unwritten law in these hills that will soon come to bear.

"While we are here talking there are men meeting in small and large groups, trying to figure out a way to feed themselves and their families. You have seen what happened when Mr. Arthur was arrested; how people ever restrained themselves then, I don't know.

"There is a strong Klan in these hills, they don't parade around in sheets, but by God, they are there. Most of them are good men and only want justice, if what you are doing to me, and a few other men that I know about is what you truly feel is justice, then take me back to jail. I have never run from trouble nor have I ever gone looking for it.

"Myrtle is alive, she left on her own, and I haven't harmed her in any way. And for this, you have taken everything I owned from me, just because you thought I had done something. Or else it is because of my hatred for that greasy-haired son of a bitch, "Grady". He is a bad man Judge and he bullies everyone he can, someday someone will kill him or beat him half to death. People believe that you put him up to most of it. This I don't know, but if this is the case it is wrong, and the day will come when you both will pay for what you are doing.

"If you will turn me loose and give me back my children, I will find work someplace and care for them. I won't go looking for Grady, but I won't be bullied by him either. I realize he was just doing his job. But someone ought to show him how to do it in a gentler manner."

Judge Brown looked over his glasses at Carl and said, "If what I heard is true, you gentled him down quite a bit.

"He didn't charge you with resisting arrest, which he had every right to do. I think maybe his deputy Clarence had something to do with that. You might want to thank him sometime. For Carl, you aren't one of Grady's favorite people either.

"I will make a few phone calls and see if I can turn you lose on your word not to leave the county. It will take a couple of days to get your children back to you. We have to know they will have a home to go to and be well cared for. I will see if I can get some of your belongings returned. And I will apologize for any wrong the county has done to you. The law doesn't always work right, but it does work. Try to remember that."

Carl was again taken back to the jail where he spent the day alone in his cell, sitting and thinking about the things he had said to the judge, something he wished he hadn't said, but by God they were the truth.

The next day he returned to work on the road with the rest of the prisoners, only this time they didn't put leg chains on him, he was free to move about and the guards never ordered him around. On Wednesday a patrol car came out and picked him up, telling him the Judge was letting him go home. He told the deputy that from what he knew, he no longer had a home to go too, that the county and the marble company had taken everything he owned.

Carl had to go in and sign some papers in front of the Judge, who again apologized to him, and gave him four dollars, saying, "I know this is little pay for weeks of working on the road but it is the best the county can do."

It was twenty miles to Phenix from Springfield, and it was getting late in the afternoon when Carl started his long walk home. He was hungry but didn't want to spend any of the money he had. Stopping at a little roadside park he drank from a spring and rested, he thought about just spending the night there, but knew he would just get hungrier, so he walked on down the road.

It was after midnight when he got to his folk's place. Grandma got up and fixed him some food. He was totally exhausted, both physically and mentally, after eating he walked into the living room and lay down on a woven rug that was on the floor. Grandma got a blanket and laid it over him. He was asleep in seconds and slept until almost noon the next day. When he awoke, he and Granddad walked over to the old hotel that he had been living in. Carl told his father that it looks like I have lost everything. Grandfather smiled and said, "Not quite. As soon as we heard about you being arrested, Grandma and I figured out what that damn Judge was up to, so we took all the canned goods, the two hogs and everything we could carry over to our house. You did lose some of the furniture, but your guns, traps and most of the kitchen stuff are in my shed. You have enough to set up housekeeping again, and the family will help."

Word went out around the hills that Carl was free; no charges had ever been formally filed against him. He had been taken and held for over ten weeks just on suspicion alone.

That Sunday a large gathering took place at my grandfather's home. His brothers, Uncle Charlie, Uncle Tom, Uncle Walt, and all their families, Aunt Lou, who is a twin to Uncle Tom, her and younger sister Alice were there with their families. There were about thirty of the Bradys present from Grandmother's side of the family. Uncle Tom had five boys and five girls they were Velma, Ella, Edna, Vivian, and Nina. The boys were Otis, Leonard, Kenneth, Howard, and Gordon. Needless to say, Otis wasn't present nor was his name ever brought up. Aunt Lou had married my grandmother's brother John Brady; they had nine children, Charles, Joseph, Lester, Millard, Susan, Lucille, Vera, Jessie, and Betty. Plus, Carl's brothers and sisters, Joe, twins Gene and Sterlin, Wilburn, Pauline, Ester, and Marie. Uncle Charlie had six children, Virgil, Leslie, Mae, Lawrence, Gladys, Cliff, and Alice Ruth. Uncle Walt not being as prolific as the others only had two children, Glen and Floyd. The little house wouldn't hold everyone so benches and tables were set up outside under the large pecan tree that shaded the house. All in all, there was well over a seventy people present, all family. The women were busy cooking and preparing food while the men sat and talked. Children were running and playing everywhere. The path to the outhouse got trampled down pretty well that day.

Everyone kept asking Carl what he was going to do. Several of them offered their homes to him, and the kids, says a few more won't make that much difference. Uncle John Brady said he was moving his family to California, that he had enough of Missouri and he urged Carl to take the kids and go with him.

After everyone had eaten, Mr. Corson, a friend of Granddad's showed up for a brief visit, he told Carl that he had a partially furnished house on his farm over North of Walnut Grove that he could move into and work on the farm to pay the rent. That his wife and he had lots of canned goods in the cellar, more than they could use, as some of the stuff had been canned several years ago and would spoil before they could eat it.

The Corson place was about five miles from Phenix, everyone agreed to come over the next Saturday and move Carl's stuff over there. Mrs. Grant, Myrtle's mother said she knew of a lady that was taking care of an old man over by Walnut Grove that was looking for a housekeeping job to pay for a place to live for herself and her son.

Carl walked over there the next day and talked to the lady. Her name was Ruby Maude (Poole) McCullough, she had just recently gotten divorced from a drunken husband, and really had two children. The girl Evelyn had been placed in one of the Judge's orphanages because Ruby couldn't give her a proper place to live. She had hidden her son Marvin from the Judge so still had him with her.

She agreed to move in with Carl and keep house for the family, for a place to live with her two children. The two of them walked over to the Corson's place which was about a mile from where Ruby was staying. The house was small but there was room for Ruby and the two children to have a bedroom of their own. They made arrangements with Mr. Corson to move in. Borrowed some cleaning stuff from them and spent the next two days cleaning up the little house. It had been used to store sacks of feed in and had mice running in every direction. Carl bought five traps and was catching mice quicker than he could empty the traps.

He stayed there at night and slept on the floor, wakening up each time he heard a trap snap, he said he caught over thirty mice that first night.

Uncle John Brady gave him a little fox terrier that they called Pooch, the little dog about tore the place apart killing mice and rats.

Saturday, several of Carl's brothers, and Uncles showed up with wagons and piled all of Carl's stuff into them. Grandmother had made a big picnic lunch and packed it in baskets, and boxes. The three wagons moved slowly up and down the hills but made it to Walnut Grove by lunchtime. They stopped by a little spring just outside of town and everyone enjoyed a good lunch and took a brief nap before going on.

It was getting late in the day by the time everything was unloaded. Joe decided to spend the night, but Uncle Charlie took Granddad and Grandma back home, Lawrence, and Cousin Virgil followed them.

The next morning Carl and Joe drove the wagon over to where Ruby was staying and moved her belongings over to the little house.

Carl, Vera, Jo Anna, and little Harve spent the next few days picking up rocks out of a field and stacking them in a fence row. Harve and the two girls were enrolled into the old butter knob school which was about a mile from the Corson place. Vera was now in the 7th grade having started to school as soon as she turned five. Jo was a couple of grades behind her. Jo had a lazy eye like Carl, and it gave her a lot of trouble. He didn't have money enough to get glasses for her so they always set her in the front row so she could see the black board, but she still had trouble.

Ruby would set with the girls by the oil lamp and help them with their reading. Vera was very sharp and learned fast. She didn't like the fact that Ruby had moved in. She still wanted her own mother, to whom she was very close, and could never understand her moving away. Lawrence Brady drove Carl and Ruby to Springfield to get Ruby's daughter Evelyn from the orphanage, she was almost three years old. Now there were six children in the little house. Don was still very sick so Grandma Keen took him to her home and cared for him. This eased the load on Ruby somewhat, but Vera didn't like her baby brother not being there. She had grown accustomed to caring for the baby and had developed a motherly instinct toward him. She looked forward to the Sunday trips over to her grandparent's house, when she could again hold her little brother.

Carl, Harve, and the girls worked long hard hours on the farm, but Mr. Corson was good to the family, giving them meat from his smokehouse and all the canned fruit and vegetables they needed. He often drove the kids to school in his wagon when he was going to town. Always buys them a stick of candy and gives it to them on his return.

Carl and Ruby seemed to get along well. And it wasn't long until she found herself pregnant. The couple got married in the little butter knob church that was across the road from the school. Half the community and lots of relatives attend the wedding and wished them well. Soon another girl was added to the Keen family, they named her Nancy Sue, she was born February 15th 1936.

Mr. Corson gave Dad an old 27 Chevrolet car. He spent most of his time working on it. Finally getting it to run, only he was scared to drive it very far, it would quit him on one big hill each time he tried to drive it to town. Sometimes the only way he could get up a long steep hill was to turn around and back up it. This would always make Ruby motion sick, so most of the times she would get out and walk to the top of the hills, with two or three of the little kids tagging along hanging onto her dress tail.

Chapter Seven

Ruby grew to dread these trips to town; Carl would throw such a cussing fit each time the old car wouldn't go up the long hill, and it scared her to death each time he would roll back to the bottom. More and more she found excuses not to go to town with him, it was a lot less stressful to just stay home with the kids.

Little Don was still having health problems so grandma kept him all the time now. Harve was nearing eight years old and was having severe kidney problems; he had a yellow look to him and couldn't hold food in his stomach. Dad had taken him to Walnut Grove to a Doctor there called Dr. Barber, he was a good family practitioner, but didn't know how to treat the young boy.

He told Carl that he needed to go to Springfield to a specialist, but there wasn't any money in the family for this type of doctor. So, Dr. Barber did the best he could and finally got Harve to where he could go back to school. One of the teachers got concerned and told Grady about the sick child. So, one morning him and a case worker showed up at the door and were going to take Harve to the Judge's orphanage where he could get proper medical attention.

Carl told them that the boy was doing fine and to get the hell off the porch before he threw them off. About that time Granddad showed up, he had been hunting and had a couple of squirrels he was going to give to Ruby for dinner. He asked Grady what he was doing there, and he told him it wasn't any of his business. The county nurse had to see that the kids were properly fed, and cared for. She went through all the cupboards in the kitchen and checked every room in the house, writing down things as she went, even going so far as to check out the outhouse.

Granddad took hold of Grady's arm and said, "Anything that concerns this family is my business. And you better find that out fast."

Grady pulled away and said, "Now I see where Carl gets his stupidity from." This angered Granddad to the point he held the shotgun tight and told Grady.

"Carl has been through enough hell to last him a lifetime, and you caused most of it. Hear me now, enough is enough. Don't lay foot on a Keen's porch ever again. For if you do it will be the last step you take, now get out of here and leave us be. And tell your damn uncle the Judge that the same goes for him."

Granddad was so angry he was shaking when he went inside. He told Dad it will be a miracle if one of us doesn't kills that red-headed bastard, if we're lucky he will drown himself in that damn Fitch's hair oil first, I think he even drinks that damn stuff. Ruby made the men a cup of hot sassafras tea, saying, "This should calm you two down a little." They walked outside and set on the porch drinking their tea and talking about President Roosevelt's new deal.

He was setting up a work project that was supposed to provide a job for every man that wanted to work. He called it the Work Progress Administration, or the WPA. No one cared what they called it as long as they could earn some money.

O'Grady was up for election again and had a good man running against him, only thing was he was a Republican, and since Roosevelt was so popular it was going to be hard for someone to beat a Democrat. Grady had a lot of support in the larger towns, like Springfield, he didn't bully people there like he did in the small communities, and the city police handled most of the problems around there. I guess he knew that too many people would get together and vote him out. He had taken a lot of children from the hill people and put them in the Judge's orphanage. Word had spread around the county about what they had done to Carl over his wife leaving him. And the deal with Mr. Arthur had angered a lot of people in Springfield. The newspaper had carried the story and for once had been on Mr. Arthur's side.

The WPA had given a lot of people jobs already and most every able-bodied man and boy that could qualify had signed up to go to work.

Carl, Joe, Granddad, Virgil, Uncle Charlie Keen and several more of the Keen family were on one road crew that was building BB county road from Walnut Grove, to Fair Grove. Most of this was all hand labor; consisting of pick and shovel work with a few wheel barrow-operators. Every time Uncle Joe would get hold of a wheel-barrow, Carl would tell him to get away from that thing; "That he didn't know anything about machinery." Then he would tell him that the reason a wheel-barrow has one wheel is that they used to have a half barrel with two handles on each end.

There was a gorilla on one end and an Irishman on the other, and the gorilla got smart and put a wheel on his end.

Joe would just look at his older brother in disgust and go on working.

Somehow the Judge got the power from the government to handle the WPA payrolls through his bank. The men were paid two dollars and twenty-five cents a day; the Judge would cash the men's checks and put their monthly pay in an envelope, holding out twenty-five cents a day for administration fees. He had no authority to do this but anyone that complained was subject to dismissal. And two dollars a day was better than nothing, so again the Judge got richer at the expense of the poor. Most of the men were so happy to again be able to buy groceries for their families that they didn't think about what the Judge was doing to them. Uncle Walt and Uncle Thomas worked in Dade County and got the full two twenty-five a day, so word soon spread through the Keen family, and to the other workers in Greene County.

There was a lot of griping among them, but most just said, "Let it go", as there wasn't any other work around. Election Day finally rolled around and the men were let off work for an hour to go vote, after a long speech from the Judge about how he and Grady had made all of these jobs available, and how they would fight for new roads to be built, and how they could keep these good jobs in the county.

The Judge stood there in the crowd, looking my Dad straight in the eye and told everyone what a good Constable Grady was, and how fair he was to people. Carl just turned his back and walked off, most of the family and a lot of their friend walked away with him, leaving the judge to talk with about ten men that Dad called a bunch of kiss asses.

Everyone gathered at Uncle Charlie's house that evening and listened to the voting results on Uncle Charlie's battery radio. The Judge had again run unopposed, but O'Grady was being beaten by a Springfield police officer named Wilson. Everyone walked home in good spirits, but most of them figured that Grady would win, even if the Judge had to rig the election.

Cousin Clarence showed up at Grandfather's house the next morning and told him he had quit the sheriff's office as he couldn't stand by and watch all the cruelty that Grady was handing out to the poor. He told Granddad that if Wilson got elected, he might try and get reinstated.

It took several days for the news to spread around the hills that O'Grady had lost the election and that they would soon have a new Sheriff.

Grady lost the election but would still be the sheriff for several more weeks, as the newly elected sheriff wouldn't get sworn in until after the first of the year. Granddad had a gold watch that he was very proud of; it had belonged to his father and was handed down to him. He needed to seed his field for a new wheat crop and didn't have money for the seed. He went to the bank and asked to borrow some money on the watch; Grady was in the bank and asked Grandfather where he got the watch. Granddad told him it wasn't any of his damn business where he got it, Grady shoved the old man in a fit of anger, Granddad was a much smaller man, and no match for the big Irishman. However, he pushed Grady back, and was taken down and handcuffed.

Bill, one of Uncle Walt's boys saw all of this and run to where Joe was working, and told him about Grady arresting his dad and putting him in handcuffs. Uncle Joe sent Bill to get Carl and headed for town. When Joe caught up with Grady, he had already turned Granddad loose but had kept his watch. Joe asked him once for his grandfather's watch and then shoved him backward. Joe was smaller than Grady he stood about five ten and weighed around two hundred and twenty pounds. Grady had Joe on the ground when Carl showed up; he grabbed Grady and slung him aside, telling Joe to quit fighting. Bob Grady's deputy showed up but was afraid to get into the fight. Carl told him to either get the hell out of there or start fighting. Bob threw his badge down and said, "He wasn't about to get killed over some has been sheriff," and walked away.

Joe was furious both at Grady and his brother. Carl finally pulled his brother away and asked Grady why he had arrested their father. He said, Granddad had stolen a watch and was trying to pawn it, and that when he asked him where he had gotten it that Granddad had told him it wasn't any of his damn business.

That he had shoved Granddad in a moment of anger. He said, he had apologized to him and turned him loose. Dad asked him where Granddad's watch was. Grady told him the Judge now had it, and was holding it for evidence until he could find out who it belonged to.

The two brothers pushed Grady aside and headed for the Judge's office, Joe asked the clerk where the judge was. The clerk told him he was in Springfield. Carl asked where the watch was that Grady had brought in, and was told that he put it in the safe, Joe told him the watch belonged to his dad and he wanted it. The clerk told him that only Grady or the Judge could give it up.

Joe asked where the safe was and if he knew how to open it. The clerk motioned toward the safe and said it isn't locked. He walked over and pulled the door open, Carl picked up their Dad's watch and asked where he could sign for it, as he didn't want to get arrested for stealing something that belonged to his Dad.

Grady came in about that time his greasy hair still messed up and several red splotches on his face. He told the clerk to give the men the watch. Carl turned to him and said, "Don't ever lay a hand on my father again, he has five sons of which I am the oldest; I don't want one of the younger boys to come gunning for you. And Grady, as soon as you lose that damn badge, I am going to settle things with you once and for all.

"I don't know what you have against me and the Keen family, and I really don't care! You cost me ten weeks out of my life, a job, and a home, and by God someday you are going to pay for it all with blood, sweat, and teeth." Pushing Grady aside the two brothers walked from the judge's office and never looked back.

Grady stood there his face puffy and red, he looked at the clerk and said, "Someday one of those men is going to push me too far."

Carl and Joe walked over to their Dad's house and gave him back his watch. Granddad was still very angry and told the boys he didn't need them settling his fights for him, that he was capable of taking care of that big redheaded bastard by himself. Joe said, "Yea Dad I know, but it sure was a good excuse for me to take a poke at him." He turned toward Dad and said, "Carl you sure as hell don't need any more trouble with him, he will lock you up and lose the damn key. He will soon be out of office and then you can whip his big ass anytime you feel tough enough to do it."

As the men turned to leave Granddad said, "But thanks anyway boys, I sure didn't want to lose that watch."

Carl was worried that Grady would serve a warrant against him and Joe for the fight with them. Several days passed and nothing happened so he quit worrying about it. With help from the Corson's and the WPA job, things were going great for him and Ruby.

They had managed to raise about fifty chickens and a couple of hogs.

Jo Anna was baking muffins and got into the large salt container instead of the sugar, needless to say, the muffins were a little salty. She fed them to the chickens and it killed all fifty of the fryers Dad had worked so hard to feed. It was a huge loss for the family as they had been expecting to can some of the meat to get through the winter. Dad swore a little and dug a huge hole and made the children pick up all the dead chickens and put them in it. Poor Jo cried for several days, Ruby tried to console her but she missed her real mother and cried for her. Vera tried hard to cheer up her younger sister but to no avail. Jo could see the hurt in her father's eyes each time she looked at him. She wanted to put her arms around his neck and tell him she was sorry, but Dad never seemed to ever give her the chance. He would come home from the WPA job so tired he could hardly walk, after eating a bite he would rest for a spell, and then work several hours on the Corson farm to pay for the rent. He was now milking all of the cows and cleaning the barns both night and morning. Mr. Corson had a son that helped him when he got home from school.

One morning cousin Virgil showed up at Carl and Ruby's house, he was so upset that he was in tears. The Judge told him he was going to take his children and put them in the orphanage until such time he could provide a better home for them. Virgil was working on the WPA but his meager wages wouldn't pay the rent on the run-down farm he was living on. The farm had once belonged to Uncle Charlie but the damn Judge had foreclosed on it after the banks closed, and now he was renting it to Virgil who was really the rightful owner.

Virgil said he didn't know what to do but there was no way he was going to let them take his children from him. He said the Judge had given him three weeks to improve the situation or they were placing six of the eight children in his orphanage. Again, the call went out to all the families around, they held another meeting at the Keel Hall. There were about seventy people showed up. Some of them had already lost their children to the Judge's orphanage, and they weren't even allowed to visit them.

Mr. and Mrs. Baker had stolen their three children back from the orphanage and fled the state with them, leaving everything they possessed behind. Friends and neighbors had cleaned out their farm and stored everything in a large barn.

The meeting lasted well into the night, it was finally decided that Virgil would have to move over to Dade County where the judge there didn't own an orphanage so wouldn't take anyone's children as he could, get paid for keeping them.

Virgil stood up and said the damn Judge can go to hell; he was selling out and going to take his family to California. He knew that the family could make more money picking fruit than he could be working for the WPA. When the meeting was over, someone noticed that Grady was standing in the doorway listening. Virgil walked up to him and told him to tell the Judge he was leaving the state and taking his children with him, and the judge could have that damn rock pile of a farm that he had been breaking his back on trying to raise a crop and shove it up his royal American ass. Carl, Joe, Uncle Charlie, and Virgil's two oldest boys were all standing behind Grady, when he turned around, he got a pale look on his face and quickly eased out of the doorway and walked to his car. No one spoke a word to him, but he could feel the tension in the air.

Chapter Eight

Nancy was less than two years old when Ruby found out that she was pregnant again. It seemed like the one thing Carl was good at was making babies. Ruby was very sick during the pregnancy, so Vera and Jo Anna were forced to do a lot of the cooking and most of the laundry, which was scrubbed by hand on a couple of old washboards. Some mornings the girls were so tired that they fell asleep in school.

Dad tried to help as much as he could, but his back was bothering him, and some mornings he went to work so stooped over that he looked like an old man. He would sleep on his back lying on the kitchen floor, trying to get it to quit hurting.

Cousin Virgil had worked out a deal with the Judge, where the rent he was paying on the farm went to the price Uncle Charlie still owed on it. So now he decided to stay and work the land, everyone was glad to hear that they weren't moving to California. Grady left the country for a while after his defeat by Sheriff Wilson. No one had seen or heard anything about him.

The work crew that Dad, Joe, and Granddad worked on had been moved over farther north to build a new bridge over the Sac River. This was a project that everyone looked forward to working on.

The first few weeks were spent clearing brush and digging down the grade so that the bridge footings for each end could be laid in place.

With Grady gone and the WPA job, Carl seemed to always be in a good mood. He loved playing practical jokes on people, there were lots of snakes in the area where the men worked, and he was always pitching one at someone. One day one of the other workers a man called Sam who kissed the boss's rear on a regular basis, was climbing up a steep muddy bank to go talk with the foreman. Dad made a mud ball and threw it at Sam, he missed and hit the foreman in the back of the head. When the foreman turned around there stood Sam with mud all over his hands and no one around. Sam tried to explain that someone else did it, but Carl and Joe were busy elsewhere. The foreman made Sam take a wheelbarrow and go shovel out ditches for the next two weeks.

One morning the men showed up for work and their new boss was there. It was no other than O'Grady himself; somehow the Judge had got him a supervisor job. He walked around and shook hands with everyone but Granddad, Joe, and Carl; he just walked past them like they weren't even there. Carl was ready to quit, Joe talked him into staying telling him he wasn't about to let that greasy-haired bastard run him off of a good job.

Granddad just smiled and said, "Maybe I can get him to check out a powder charge one of these days."

Carl was a hard worker, he couldn't stay still for very long, and few men could keep up with him no matter what he was doing. When he was home, he was always working on the Corson farm. Mr. Corson told him that he didn't need to work that hard around there but Carl had a drive in him that always kept him busy. (Maybe this was why he fathered so many children). My son seems to be afflicted with this same work ethic. Somehow it skipped my generation. (Lucky Me).

Dad bought Ruby a gas-powered washing machine, this made doing the wash a lot easier, even though they still had to heat the water outside over an open fire. Ruby was scared to let the girls run the clothes through the old hand-turned wringer, she was afraid one of them would get their hand caught in it, but she would have the girls turn the crank while she fed the wet clothing through it.

##############

Grady left Joe and Carl alone, he seldom told them what he wanted done, having someone else pass the word to them. Grady did have one of the men mow his lawn and the judge's place also. At times there would be two or three men working on one of the Judge's farms while being paid by the government. It was said that the only way some of the men kept their jobs was the fact that their wives done the Judge's laundry for him and cleaned his house.

Everyone that worked on the WPA had to be careful that their children didn't get into any fights with Grady's kids or anyone related to the judge. These men lived in fear of losing the only job around, for there was always someone lurking around trying to get their job. People snuck around and took pictures of men leaning on a shovel or goofing off. They would even buy jobs when there was one open. Granddad was the only powder man around, as most folks were afraid of dynamite, and didn't want anything to do with it.

Ruby was overdue with the baby and the doctor was worried about the size of the child. On May 1st 1938, a boy was born to her and Carl, he weighed twelve pounds and eleven ounces. They named him Karl David Keen, as Ruby wanted him to be a preacher. (Wrong again) having such a large baby gave Ruby a hernia that bothered her for many years, as they never had enough money for an operation. Shortly after the baby was born, Mr. Carson's son Thornton announced that he was getting married and wanted the little house.

So, Carl and Ruby with eight children were looking for a place to move to. Once again, he rented the old hotel at Phenix. His brother Sterlin and his wife Juanita rented two rooms upstairs, they only stayed about six months as there was no way to heat those rooms. The two oldest girls Vera and Jo Anna slept in a room downstairs in the front part of the hotel, this room had been used as a barber shop when the hotel was in operation. It had a large picture window in front, and the girls didn't have anything to cover it with completely. One night as they were getting ready for bed, Vera walked over to blow out the kerosene lamp and let out a blood-curdling scream, there was someone looking in the window at them. Both girls fled to Carl and Ruby's room.

Dad told them to get back to bed and that they were imagining things; about that time, he almost jumped out of his drawers for there was a face plastered to his bedroom window. He ran outside but no one was there. Vera and Joanna grabbed their blankets and moved upstairs sleeping that night on the floor. Carl was a little shaken by the whole thing and walked over to his father's house. They two had seen someone looking into their window on more than one occasion. On checking with the neighbors, it seemed like everyone in town had spotted someone either looking through their windows or just lurking about in their yard after dark.

The whole community was now upset. Men took turns walking around what was left of the little town at night, trying to catch whoever it was, often fleeting glances were caught off a figure dressed in a long coat going around a comer, or ducking into the brush. Grown men were filled with fear as more and more episodes of the night stalker were reported.

It was everyone's suspicion that it was just some old bum looking for a handout. Many times during the day, hoboes would come from the railroad tracks and bum a meal from my Mother. She never once turned a hungry soul away. Even though we verily had enough to feed us. A lot of the time the hoboes would chop wood, rake the yard, or pull weeds from the garden for their meal.

It wasn't long until the whole community was terrorized by the night stalker. Kids were afraid to go to the outhouse alone, and the older boys would hide and scare people on the way to one. Many times after a good scare, folks realized they no longer needed to go to the bathroom after being scared by someone. This was great fun for the older boys, as no one knew who they were. One night, a loud shotgun blast sent a scream up from a young prankster, and our cousin Charles has a backside full of bird shots. Lucky for him he had on a new pair of overalls and was in tall weeds that slowed down the blast.

However, it took his mom several hours to pick the shot from his backside, and the alcohol she put on it made him scream even louder.

This ended the outhouse capers, but the night stalker kept appearing at different folks' windows. One evening, Joe Keen and Lawrence Brady were walking home from a church social, and saw a figure peeking into a window, they gave chase and caught this elderly woman that was somewhat deranged. (As you would say today, her elevator didn't quite go to the top floor). She was taken home to her family. This ended the night stalkers' reign over Phenix, and once again the little community returned to its quiet way of life. Not to say people out alone at night didn't keep a good look behind them as they walked along in the dark, and few children would even go to the outhouse alone after dark.

But the older boys still pulled pranks on people. One of their favorite tricks was for all of them to sit in the front row at church on Sunday evenings. Just when the preacher would get all wound up, they would get up one at a time and walk out of the church in the middle of the service. One particular night it was one of the Keen boys' turn to go first.

They had been working on one wall of the church and a small pile of lumber was laying in the edge of the isle.

Gene got up and sauntered down the aisle with his hands in his pockets, he turned and looked back at the preacher, tripping over the pile of lumber and landing flat on his face, he jumped up and ran from the church, as it erupted in loud laughter from the congregation. The rest of the boys were so embarrassed for him they set through the whole sermon. This put an end to them walking out of church in the middle of a sermon. (God does indeed work in mysterious ways.)

###############

My sister Evelyn was about eight years old, and every time someone knocked on the door, she would holler come in. One evening just before dark we were all playing a game in the front room of the hotel, when someone knocked on the door, Evelyn hollered come in, and as the door opened there stood the ugliest old hobo any one had ever seen, kids went running and screaming in every direction (except toward the door).

All of this hollering and screaming was too much for the old bum, the last we seen of him he was going up the road at a dead run. Our mother laughed until she cried, we even got a chuckle out of Dad, and Evelyn quit hollering come in whenever someone knocked.

##############

There were now a total of eight kids in the family, with four more yet to come. My folks also raised two of my cousins and My Mom's Mother who was practically blind lived with us for many years. I guess it was a case of the more the merrier. There never seemed to be enough of anything to go around. We slept three and four to a bed.

There was never enough room or chairs to seat everyone at the table. And there always seemed to be an extra mouth or two to feed at mealtime. So, we always had a table in a side room with benches to set on. When we had visitors that stayed overnight, Mom would put a blanket on the floor for the kids to sleep on, she called this a pallet (seemed like a dang hard floor to me). But they always made room for anyone that showed up.

Dad was always bringing home some buddy of his to stay with us. Why Mom put up with this I will never know.

One thing for sure was, none of them ever paid their way. And most of them were too lazy to even carry in a stick of wood or a bucket of coal, let alone chop any wood. The old hotel had plenty of rooms in it; some were awfully cold in the winter.

##############

There was a big barn out back with a large hay loft in it. A chicken house with a nearby smokehouse that was used for curing meat. We didn't have refrigeration so all the pork was smoke and sugar cured, then hung in the smokehouse; it was covered with a salt brine and would keep through the hottest weather. There was a large crock of sugar and salt mixture that was kept close by, anytime meat was cut from a ham or side meat the fresh cut was rubbed over with this mixture to seal it.

##############

We never had electricity and batteries were too expensive to play the radio, as it took twenty-four batteries to operate it. One of the Men Dad brought home to stay with us played the guitar. This was my first introduction to music. I can't remember how well he played but we would sit on the floor around him and sing all of the songs that he could play. Being I was only about two years old I don't think I sang much. We would all go over to Uncle Charlie's on Saturday nights and listen to the grand old opera on his radio set.

There would be singing and dancing on summer evenings, as I have said before my father had a beautiful voice as well as did his sisters, they would sing for hours. Some of these get-togethers would bring people from miles around. Kids would be bedded down on blankets nearby and food would be plentiful with tables stacked full. A lot of the people stayed the night and slept on the ground or in their vehicles. The next morning a large breakfast would be cooked outside over an open fire, after breakfast, everyone headed home and did their chores, then returned for church services that evening. Some folks dozed a little during the sermon, and when the preacher would see their heads drooping, he would raise his voice real loud which would usually cause the person to look up, then look around to see if anyone had caught them sleeping.

Chapter Nine

My older brothers Harve, Jo Anna, and Vera all went to the high school at Walnut Grove. They were always harassed by the kids that lived in town and thought they were a little better than the country kids. Eddie was the oldest son of the O'Gradys and just as big a bully as his father. He was a big fat kid with a face full of pimples, his hair was the color of a carrot and his brain was just about as large. He loved to shove kids off of their bicycles when they rode by him. It seemed like he was always mad at everyone. He was constantly beating on some small kid or kicking someone for no reason. Even the teachers were afraid of him, maybe it was because of his father, or his uncle the judge.

He would walk up behind the girls and grab them by both breasts, they would try and slap him but he would just run and laugh. The girls were afraid to tell the principal or the authorities because of Mr. O'Grady being the Forman on the WPA where their fathers worked; they were in constant fear of them losing their jobs. Everyone put up with Eddie and his Brother Jimmy's abuse. They stole bicycles and anything they wanted. The merchants in town would look the other way while they stole candy and other small items.

Eddie didn't like my brother Harve; if he needed a reason, I guess it was because he was a Keen. It was their freshman year in high school and the older kids were allowed to go down

"

to the store in Walnut Grove for lunch. The store was only two blocks from the school, and the merchants had bologna and cracker for the kids for a nickel. The school never had a hot lunch program at that time, so it was either bring your lunch or buy it at one of the grocery stores.

Harve and some of his friends walked down to the store for lunch. Fat Eddie followed them down there, he kept calling Harve names and pushed him from behind. Harve took this all in stride, he bought his crackers, and bologna plus a bottle of pop. The boys were setting on the curb in front of the store eating their lunch. Eddie walked over and kicked over Harve's bottle of soda. He just stood there and laughed as the soda spilled all over the sidewalk. Harve was a small skinny kid with sunken eyes and the gaunt look of the undernourished depression kids, there wasn't a gram of fat on his body, what muscle he had was hard, gained from picking rocks, digging fence post holes, milking cows, and pitching hay. It wasn't big bulky muscle but hard-earned strength that most farm boys possessed.

Without saying a word, he stood up and hit Eddie straight in the nose, his head flew back and for a moment an expression of pure surprise come over his face, a small trickle of blood started running down his lip from the right nostril. Before he could react, Harve hit him again just over the left eye, and bloodshot forth from a nasty cut in fat Eddie's eye eyebrows was beaten before the fight ever got started. He backed up against the store, screaming and holding both hands to his face as blood ran down between his fingers, the man from the grocery store ran out and scolded Harve, telling him to leave Eddie alone.

He took Eddie back into the store and cleaned him up. Harve knew he was in trouble for fighting, as he had been told not to fight with any of Grady's children because it would be a sure way for Carl to lose his job. When he got back to school, he was sent immediately to the principal's office, as word of the fight got back to school before he did.

The principal told him to come into his office and set down; he got up and closed the door not saying anything to Harve, just leaving to him set there to agonize over his fate. After setting there shifting through a stack of papers, the principal looked up over his glasses and asked Harve what took place downtown between him and Eddie. He tried to explain to the principal how Eddie had been calling him names and picking on him for some time, and when he kicked over his soda it was the last straw. The Principal severely reprimanded Harve telling him that fighting would not be allowed in school or by any of the students on or off the school grounds.

Harve just sat there with his head down, not looking at the principal. He was more worried about what his father was going to do to him, than he was the principal. He was told to sit there in the principal's office the rest of the day, and to think about what he had done. Tears came to the young boy's eyes as he looked up at the principal and said, "Yes sir." Harve wished he hadn't hit Eddie even though he did think Fat Eddie had it coming. He had to smile at himself when he remembered how loud it popped when he punched him in the nose, and the look of surprise that come over Eddie's face, he just couldn't believe that someone had finally smacked him.

Like most bullies, Eddie thought that he could always get by with pushing and mistreating people and nothing would ever happen to him, well by golly he sure got the surprise of his life. Harve was really scared of Eddie but the thought of him spilling his lunch soda on purpose was more than he could take. The more he thought about it, the better he felt about what he had done. He was sure to get a whipping from his Dad when he got home, he had been told about fighting and also about leaving the Grady kids alone.

Would this cost his father his job? The thought worried him the rest of the day. And what about Eddie, would he come looking for revenge, or would Grady come and arrest him, even though he was no longer the constable?

When the bell rang for the end of the school day he hated to get on the bus and ride the three miles to Phenix. Kids tried to ask him about the fight but he was too sick to talk about it. When the bus stopped in front of the hotel he hated to get off. He walked into the hotel going straight to the bedroom that he shared with Marvin, and Don. He changed his clothes and went straight out to the wood pile and started cutting wood. Not even taking time to say hi to his stepmom Ruby. With each swing of the axe, he became more upset, until he was nearly in tears by the time his father got home from work. Carl came out of the house and walked over to where he was working; he took one look at him and asked what was wrong. Harve burst into tears and told him all about hitting Eddie. Carl took his young son into his arms and told him not to worry, that the worse thing about it was he hadn't been there to see it. Then he explained to him about fighting, that he did have a right to protect himself, but was it worth if over a bottle of pop. Harve said to him it was, as the pop was almost full, he had only taken one sip, and that it would be weeks before he could ever save up two more pennies for another one.

Dad ran his hand through the boy's hair, and said, "Let's get in some wood and see if Ruby has supper ready yet."

Harve felt a load off his mind but was still worried about his Dad losing his job, only he was afraid to ask about it. No one said much during dinner, and the fight wasn't brought up again that day. Harve wished it was Saturday so that he didn't have to go back to school. He pretended that he was sick the next day and Ruby let him stay home, even though she did threaten to give him a spoon full of castor oil.

The next day he got on the bus with the Brady kids and Uncles Virgil's boys, they were telling him about the black eye that Fat Eddie had. This he didn't really want to hear about. He just wanted to stay away from Eddie and avoid any more trouble. Everyone at school was slapping him on the back and telling him what a good thing he had done. Well, he sure didn't feel like it was a good thing. And when Eddie came into the room his eye looked terrible, Harve couldn't believe he had done that to someone. He got up and walked over to Eddie and told him he was sorry. This took everyone by surprise even big Eddie. He finally squeaked out, it's ok; I guess I was asking for it.

The teacher came into the room about then and made everyone sit down; she looked at Harve and told him that she believed he owed Eddie an apology. Harve told her he had already apologized to Eddie. After that, things sort of returned to normal. Except everywhere Harve went, Eddie followed him, he wanted to be friends, it was amazing how one black eye turned Eddie into a likable person, and away from the bully he had always been.

############

Carl sure wasn't looking forward to going to work either, for he had already lost one job for fighting with Grady. And he just knew that Grady would fire him or give him ever nasty job that could be found. He told Joe about the fight between Harve and Eddie. Joe just laughed and said, "He was glad someone finally smacked that spoiled little bastard."

Grady was late showing up on the job that day and it sure turned Carl's stomach when he drove up. He just busied himself with his work and never looked at Grady. The day went fast and Grady never spoke a word to him. Now he was really worried, wondering what was going to happen. Granddad told him to forget it, that this was a government job, and it would be hell for Grady to try and fire someone just because their kids had a fight.

The next day Grady came over to where Carl was working and said, "I hear that boy of your packs a mean right hand." Carl just stood there looking at him not knowing what to say. Grady smiled, rubbed his chin, and said, "He must get it from his old man." Turning to leave he slapped Carl on the shoulder and walked across the bridge.

Carl just stood there, looking up at Joe, and said, "You know! That big red-headed bastard just might be part human."

Both men laughed and continued their work.

##############

Granddad was down below the men working on a plugged culver when someone heard him holler, and he came running up the bank with a big raccoon right on his heels, he grabbed a shovel from one of the men and struck it knocking it down, another blow from the shovel dispatched it. Granddad started to pick it up when Grady hollered, "Don't touch it."

Granddad looked at him, and Grady said, "I think that coon is mad." Granddad laughed and said, "He sure as hell was, he's so damn mad he tried to bite me."

Grady said, "I mean it might have hydrophobia." Everyone stepped back and stared at him. They call it rabies back east. There isn't anything more dangerous than a mad dog, they will bite and snap at everything, and they just go blind and crazy.

Grady told Granddad to go down to the river and wash his hands good, as he had been working where that rabid coon had been. Several men followed Granddad down to the river and washed. They picked the coon up with a shovel and buried it.

Grady called everyone together and told them to be aware of any animal they came across, and for them all to wash well before eating lunch. He had the men to work in another area, and told them to stay away from the culvert that the rabid coon had come from. The men were really jumpy the rest of the day. Carl and Joe had fun goosing men with sticks, or rubbing one against the back of their legs, several of the men would jump and holler anytime something touched them.

When Carl got home from work he told Ruby about the rabid coon, and told her to keep a close watch on the kids and to beware of any dogs that got to acting strange or were foaming at the mouth.

Ruby had heard of mad dogs and of people getting bit by them, and the horror stories of them being chained to a tree while they died of hydrophobia. How they screamed and bit at everything and cried for water, and not being able to swallow when it was given to them. Ruby kept all of the smaller children in the house and when the school bus came, she hollered for the older kids to run to the house. She set them all down and explained to them about mad dogs, and other animals that might have rabies.

Harve and the two younger boys were afraid to go get the cows into milk. He carried Granddad'sold twelve-gauge shotgun to the barn with him. The cows all ran on open range, so the boys had to go round them up, and bring them to the barn at milking time.

Dad had just bought a milk cow from our neighbor Mrs. Cristman, the old cow still thought she belonged over there so every day when it was time to be milked, she would show up at the Cristman's back door. They had a little Boston bulldog that didn't like anyone, now Harve was extra scared of it now, since he was afraid of it having rabies, he would always take our big collie with him when he would go over there to get the cow.

The little bulldog was afraid of the bigger dog and would stand back and bark at her. They also had a son that wasn't right in the head; he would take off his clothes and run outside hollering at any girl that went by. All of my sisters and a lot of the grown women were afraid of him. Sometimes he would just stand in front of the window naked and holler at people. Mrs. Cristman did the best she could with him, but he was now a teenager and very strong. Mr. Cristman had died and she was now alone to try and handle the boy. Several times Dad or one of his brothers would go over and calm him down and make him put his clothes back on.

The boy started getting out of the house at night and running around the town. People were becoming scared of him; afraid he would attack some women or little girl. So, the law finally came and took him to an asylum. This broke Mrs. Cristman's heart, as he was the only child they ever had, and he was born to them late in life.

My sister Nancy and I were playing out in the front yard when Ruby let out scream and just stood there, coming toward us was a mad dog, it was staggering and foaming at the mouth. Ruby couldn't seem to move she was so scared. Finally, she grabbed both of us and ran into the house closing all the doors and windows. She was deathly afraid of guns and didn't want one in the room with her. She had never fired a gun or even picked one up, so I doubt if she would have known which end the bullet come out of, even if she could get one loaded.

All of the older kids were in school and it was about time for them to get home. Ruby was afraid to open the door and she stood there and cried until she saw the bus, she ran out on the porch screaming as soon as the kids started getting off the bus. Mr. Wheeler the bus driver jumped out of the bus and ran to the porch trying to find out what was wrong. Ruby was so scared she couldn't tell him about the mad dog, she just cried and mumbled as she pushed all the scared kids into the house.

Mr. Wheeler finally got her calmed down enough to learn what had her so upset. He took Dad's shotgun and walked down to the creek where he found the dog lapping up water. It seemed to be all right to him as it came right up, and didn't act strange at all, following him back up to the house. The dog belonged to Mr. Taylor one of the other neighbors, he came over and Ruby told him of how it was foaming at the mouth and staggering when it came into the yard. The bus driver gave him Dad's shotgun and left. Mr. Taylor examined the dog then walked up the road to where a small drainage ditch ran along the road, he came back laughing and told Ruby about her mad dog.

The dog had killed a large toad frog, which has bitter-tasting oil on its skin to protect itself, this was why the dog was slobbering and foaming at the mouth, the reason it was staggering was the fact it kept pawing at its mouth with its foot, trying to get the taste out of it.

Ruby was so embarrassed over her mad dog incident that she didn't want to talk about it, but it left her with a fear of mad dogs for the rest of her life.

Chapter Ten

Ruby's episode with the rabid dog wasn't for nothing. As the coon Granddad killed must have been rabid. It seemed like every fox, rabbit, and dog in the country soon was inflicted. People carried guns where ever they went, our neighbor, Mr. Chapman went out to feed his chickens as he reached into the feed bin a rat jumped up and bit him on the nose. He was able to kill it and had it checked, it tested positive for rabies and he had to take a series of shots that were given to him in the naval. I guess the procedure was quite painful, but he survived, even though I did see him go mad a couple of times.

Soon the rabies epidemic ran its course, and everything eventually returned to normal.

##############

Our cousin had an old Billy goat that would get out and chase anyone that would run from it. My brothers used to ride past and kick at him; he would chase them all over the place on their bicycles. My sisters were afraid to go outside, so Dad went over and had a talk with him. He pinned up the old goat, one day my sister and I were running back and forth with a stick rubbing it on the fence and teasing it. When we came to the gate, it was open and the goat was after us and we ran screaming for home. Our two dogs, a big collie and a little fox terrier came to our rescue, the old collie grabbed that goat by the throat as the fox terrier had it by a back leg. The goat was blatting something fierce and the dogs kept hanging on and shaking it until it either had a heart attack or they killed it. I was really scared as I watched my sister drag it into the weeds at the edge of the road. Everyone thought a car had hit it. When Dad found it, he dragged it over to Mr. Higgins place and threw it in his yard. He complained about smelling like that old goat for several days. We never heard another word about it, so I guess Mr. Higgins thought a car had killed it.

##############

When I was three years old, we moved a couple of houses down the street, to what was known as the old Claypool home. There was a large spring that ran out of the hillside and into the creek. Dad had dug the spring out and we kept milk and butter in it in large gallon fruit jars with the lids tightly sealed, placing a rock on top to keep them from floating around. Every once in a while, there would be a minnow or crawfish show up in the milk jug, no one seemed to ever know how they got in there, being kids we wouldn't want to drink the milk which always made Dad angry, he would always tell us that the spring water we drank had fish and crawfish in it, so what was the difference? Somehow it just didn't taste as good after you had seen something swimming in it.

##############

The old Claypool house had a large porch running around the back and along each side. Mom always kept the washing machine on the porch and they would build a fire nearby and heat the wash water. One day I wandered off and walked into the pile of hot coals where the fire had been. I fell and severely burnt my hands and feet; the Doctor told my folks that I probably would never walk again as the bums were so bad that they burned the tendons in my feet. They had to wrap each finger separately so that they wouldn't grow together. And if this didn't add enough to the family problems, Mom soon found out that she was pregnant again.

I guess I healed up ok as I don't have any remembrance of this, and I don't have any scars from it.

#############

The WPA and other government jobs seemed to be helping people get on their feet. As families tried to get their children from the orphanage, the judge was charging them a hundred dollars a child for them to get their kids back. At two dollars a day it was impossible for most people to raise that kind of money. Men were going to the law but no one would help them, several people stole their children back or else the kids just ran away and went home. They didn't go to school as their parents kept them hid. Afraid that they would be taken away again, this caused a lot of kids to miss out on getting an education.

A bunch of the families met one evening at my grandfather's place, there was a lot of talk about just going over and taking all the children from the orphanage and burning it down. However, there were children that had nowhere else to go. My Mom kept telling everyone to write to their political leaders, but she was just laughed at, they said it was the damn politicians that were running the places. And they figured every one of them was making money off of those children. Young men were being worked like slaves on the farms and being charged more for room and board than the judge was paying them, so they were always in debt to him.

Several of the young girls had been molested, but no one would believe them, these children lived in mortal fear. Most of them ran away when they got old enough to go on their own.

Anyone that complained soon found themselves out of a job, as Grady still did the judge's dirty work for him.

Christmas was the worse time of year for the kids and their parents, sometimes visits were allowed, but they weren't allowed to give the children a gift unless it was opened by one of the staff first. Any food taken to them was quickly whisked away to be eaten by the staff or someone else. The county had strict control and the crooked officials, and workers at the orphanages weren't about to let anyone find out what was going on there.

Young girls that ran away told terrible stories of being molested, and of having to dress, and undress as well as bathe in front of men that were supposed to be their guardians. Many of the young boys had been sexually molested also but most of them were too ashamed to admit what had happened to them. It was believed that the old judge knew what was going on but did little to try and stop it.

The women of the community got together and wrote letters to the governor and other state and federal officials. They were afraid to sign their names, in fear of their husbands being fired from their jobs.

The Governor however kept getting many letters from the area that was unsigned. All criticizing the judge and his orphanage, some mentioned how he was siphoning wages from the men that worked on the WPA, they kept asking the Governor to check into the matter. Especially where the children were being molested and the fact people had to pay to get their children back.

One morning a new man named Frank showed up on the work crew with Carl and Granddad, he told them he had moved down from Jefferson City to Walnut Grove to care for his ailing mother. Neither man knew the woman mentioned but thought little of it.

Grady took offense to a new man being sent to him; he gave the man every dirty job that he could think up. Frank took each job assignment to heart, and smiled as he worked, he tried to get Granddad to teach him about explosives but Grady wouldn't hear of it.

Come payday Frank asked Carl about the shortage on his check, Carl told him the judge held out twenty-five cents a day for administrative fees. Frank became friendly with my father even staying with us for a while. Ruby did his laundry and cooked meals for him. He finally rented a room from Mrs. Christian who lived next door to us. Ruby continued to wash his clothes. He and Carl rode to work together, picking up Joe and Granddad on the way.

He soon fit right in with everyone in the community, he loved to sing and dance Carl and Frank, along with Lawrence Brady, and Joe Keen formed a barbershop quartet. They would sing at all the community affairs and at church every Sunday, even singing on the local radio station in Springfield. Frank could do a few magic tricks which thrilled the little kids, and he loved to ask questions and try to get the kids to guess the answers. We spent many evenings sitting around the old coal stove trying to guess his riddles. He knew the capitals of every state and talked about far-off places that most of us in the Missouri Hills had never heard of. My father often spoke of how well he was educated and wondered why he was working on the WPA?

Frank tried to visit a boy in the orphanage that was supposed to be his nephew. Many times he was turned down when he went to visit. One time he was asked to pay five dollars to see the boy. He paid and asked for a receipt. This made the people at the orphanage mad and they told him to leave and never come back.

It wasn't long until Frank was friends with almost everyone that had children in the orphanage. He would take folks in his car every Saturday and Sunday to visit their children, often spending all day there. For a man that had a sick mother to care for, he never seemed to go to Walnut Grove very often. Joe told him about the trouble Carl had with Grady and the Judge and about the men that were forced to work on the judge's farms for being drunk, and how men were sent from the work crews to harvest crops for the judge. Frank became more and more concerned about what was going on.

He asked Joe and Carl if they would testify in court about the things he'd seen and what had happened to them. Finally, he explained to them that he was from the Governor's office, and that he had been sent down here to investigate some of the complaints the governor had gotten about the Judge and O'Grady. He asked them not to tell anyone until he could gather more evidence about all the wrong doing.

At the dances and social events, Frank would talk to people about the judge and his nephew Grady. A lot of the men were afraid to say anything. Being afraid that it would get back to the wrong people and they would lose their jobs. Frank got to where he would push Grady every day trying to see what he would make him do. One day he sent him to the Judge's farm and made him work there for two weeks building a fence. The fence was supposed to be along the county road, but Frank ended up building cross fences for the judge using wire and post that came from the road project. The wire and post were supplied by the government. This was just the kind of things Frank was looking for. He told Carl that he would soon be moving back to Jefferson City but that another man from the Governor's office would be down to carry on where he left off.

On Monday, Frank brought a man named Smith over and introduced him to Carl and Joe. They called him Smitty, he moved into the room at Mrs. Christian's house where Frank was living. Smitty was just the opposite of Frank, he liked to talk to people and was at our house every time they weren't at work. He took most of his evening meals with us, it was the few times we had steak. Smitty would buy a big package of meat for Mom to cook. It was welcome to us from the salt pork and chicken we usually ate.

Smitty was well-liked by O'Grady and they spent a lot of time talking about fishing and hunting with Grady's fox hounds.

My Mom hated fox hunters, she always said that they were a lazy bunch, that all they did was stand by a fire all night, drink whiskey, and tell lies to each other. Then sleep all day so they could do it again the next night. She would go on about how they would let their crops rot in the field and their farms go to ruin while they spent all of their time fox hunting.

Chapter Eleven

In the comer of Greene, Polk, and Dade counties of southwest Missouri, lies some of the best fox hunting in the state. Most people around the little community of Phenix, Walnut Grove, Ash Grove, and Everton, either own Fox hounds or knows someone that does. Men that could verily feed their families didn't think anything of paying several hundred dollars for a good fox hound. They always seem to have something to trade or sell to raise money.

During the Depression years, men spent a lot of time standing around fires at night listening to their hounds run. This seemed to release the stress of being unemployed and gave them something in common with one another. A lot of men trapped the rivers for raccoons and muskrats, as did my father and grandfather, if they caught a fox, it was quickly turned loose or else kept very quiet. Hay stacks and barns have been burned because of people killing a fox.

Most of the fox hounds at this time were of the walker breed or a cross with a plot, or a mixed breed of a walker and blue tick. Some dogs were bread just to hunt coons but the fox hunters wouldn't have anything to do with a coon dog. They didn't want one around the country where they hunted.

On most any cold clear night you could hear a pack of hounds running, it was music to the hill folk's ears. People would set outside at night and listen to dogs run; it got to where some folks could tell who was hunting by the sound of their hounds. When a hound hit a trail, he would let out a deep guttural bawl that would be shortly answered with another bawl as he sniffed the trail. Once a hot scent was struck the bawling would continue as one long bawls after another, usually followed by the owk, owk, owk of another dog and the yelk, yelk call of a turkey-mouthed hound. Men could distinguish their dog's bark from any other at a great distance. Dogs were bred just for the bawling sounds they made when running a fox. As I stated before my mother hated fox hunters and wouldn't let any of the boys own a fox hound. My older brothers would slip out at night and listen to the hound run if they were nearby. As a small child, I loved to hear the chopping owk, owk, owk, that a hound would make when running a hot trail.

I would sit and listen to the men talk about their dogs. Uncle Virgil had two hounds, one named General Lee and the other Stonewall after Stonewall Jackson. General Lee was a large black and white walker hound with a few brown splotches on him; he was an older dog and had a deep bass-bawling voice that rang through the valleys when he was trailing a fox. Stonewall as Uncle Virgil called him was a smaller dog about the same color but had a little blue tick in him. The white on his sides was spotted with blue dots, he was a long-legged hound that could run all night, his voice wasn't as deep as General Lee's, and he had what was called a turkey voice that was more of a yelping sound.

Our neighbor Mr. Weaver had several hounds, he always named them after military people. There was an old walker hound named Major; Captain was a big Walker hound he called, "Cap", and one old hound was named Sarge. There was a little female he called Queen; Weaver raised several litters of pups from her. He always kept this dog with him everywhere he went. Some folks say she slept on the bed beside him, and I don't doubt it, as the relationship of these hounds' men had with their dogs was very strong.

Once a good running fox was found the hunters would run it for hours. Some foxes loved to play with the hounds just running fast enough to stay ahead of the pack, they would lead dogs up and down hills and through river bottoms in circles for several hours before they would tire and lose the dogs. Either by denning up or swimming across a river back and forth until the dogs could no longer get their scent.

Every fox hunter had an old bull horn that he used at feeding time; they would stand and blow through it making a long bellowing sound. This would alert the dogs to feeding. And at night when they wanted the hounds to quit running, they would blow the horns and the dogs would come in from the chase. Each horn made a different sound and the dogs would only come to their owner's call.

I was probably four years old when I went with my father and Uncle Virgil, along with several other men on a fox hunt at night. It was down between Phenix and Ash Grove along the banks of Clear Creek. A large fire was built and a few logs dragged up to set on, I don't remember seeing the hounds, so they must have been released someplace along the river. This was a farming country with small farms scattered out all along the creek. My Dad wrapped his huge coat around me and held me tight as we set and watched the fire burn.

I can't remember how long we had been there when Mr. Weaver jumped to his feet and said, "They've struck a trail", I can hear Queen talking to him. From a far distance, I could hear the long wailing, warble voice of a dog piercing the cold clear night, I remember clinging tightly onto Dad, and him telling me not to be scared that they wouldn't hurt me, for they had only found the trail of a fox. He told me to listen and I would soon hear more dogs join the chase. Soon I could hear the owk, owk, owk, and the deep bawling of two more dogs. As they come closer more hounds blended their voices into a beautiful sound that was like bugles blowing in the night.

All the men except Dad were on their feet, calling out the names of their hounds as the fox led them along the river bank and back up over Bunker Hill, until the sound of their bugling voices could verily be heard.

Everything became quiet as the men sat down and poured coffee from a bucket they had hanging over the fire. It smelled good but Dad wouldn't let me have any, he did give me an apple he was carrying in his pocket. I set there chewing on the apple looking at all the men, I can still see their weathered faces, but the years have erased the memories of what they looked like from my mind. I am sure if I could see them again, I could remember who they were, especially, "Mr. Weaver and Uncle Virgil."

I became sleepy and Dad laid me in the seat of Mr. Weavers car, he covered me with his coat and left the door open so that I could hear the hounds if they came back. The next thing I remember was wakening up to the sound of men blowing those bull horns, and Dad asking me if I was ready to go home.

I must have slept all the way home for I can't remember anymore about that night. I do remember talking about it the next morning at breakfast, and Mom scolding Dad for keeping me out all night with a bunch of nasty-talking fox hunters. I asked Dad when we could go with Uncle Virgil again and this brought some more words from Mom about me growing up to becoming a shiftless no account.

I would lay awake at night and listen trying to hear a pack of hounds, the hoot owls, and whippoorwills would call from along the creek, mixed with the loud bellows of bullfrogs, and the cheeping of the small tree frogs. Some nights I could catch the far-off guttural baying of a hound as he sniffed out the trail of another fox. I would drift off to sleep dreaming of the campfire and the excitement of the men as their dogs chased the fox along the river banks, each one of them calling out a dog's name, as the night air was split by the ringing of a baying hound, they all sounded almost alike to me.

I always looked forward to the visits we had with Mr. Weaver, especially when he would tell of his dogs and the chases they had made. I remember him telling of a ghost fox that was nearly all white except for the red tail and a red spot on the top of its head and shoulders. It was exceptionally large for a fox, some folks claimed he was crossed with a mongrel dog; others just said he was an albino or mutant fox. One that happens in every million or so litter.

This fox was what is known as an endurance runner, he wouldn't den up as most foxes do when they become tired. The ghost fox was built to run and run he did, he would run all night or until the hounds were too exhausted to chase him. Many hunters had seen him in the moonlight, they all said he was nearly as tall as a hound and was sleek as a race horse.

The hunters got to where they wouldn't lose all their dogs at once, holding them back until the run was a couple of hours old then they would turn four or five hounds loose that were fresh to continue the chase. All this ever did was prolong the chase until everything would go quiet and the dogs would come in too exhausted to run anymore.

This just added fuel to the story of the ghost fox, as he would lose a pack of twenty hounds like he had wings. There were stories of him grabbing a stick of wood and holding in his mouth while he floated down the river past the hounds, the wood just holding his nose above water.

Some men claimed he would climb a tree and jump out onto a rock bluff that was too steep for the hounds to climb.

There was another fox that was reported to have been seen in the Sac River country that had one white side, many hunters claimed this was the ghost fox; they called it old white sides, it too was an endurance runner. The Sac river packs as the hounds in that area were called ran this fox for several years. Whether the two animals were the same or could have been litter mates will never be known. No one had ever seen both animals, but from the description that was given of them, they were entirely two different foxes.

The Ghost fox ran mostly around Clear Creek or over into the Asher Creek drainage which was several miles away. Clear Creek did run into Sac River, so their ranges did overlap. Some people believed that the fox both ran together and one would lead the chase for several miles and the other fox would come in and lead the hounds off. I don't believe a fox is that smart, but I guess it could happen by accident.

The fox hunters were afraid someone would trap the fox just to get the part of white skin; one farmer let it be known that he had set traps for the fox. Several rows of his corn were tramped down, and they let it be known that if he killed the white fox he would have empty corn cribs the next winter.

I never got to go with my father on any more hunts, I doubt if he ever went again, knowing how my Mom felt about fox hunters. As I grew up, I did hunt coons with Mr. Weaver's sons, men that I am still friends with today.

The ghost fox or white sides which ever you want to call them, gave many hours of pleasure to the area fox hunters and the dogs they owned. There were dogs traded and dogs stolen. Men were known to fight over how their dogs performed, and for degrading another man's hound. There was one killing I know of over the disappearance of a hound.

This story was written about in a book called The Voice of Bugle Ann, which later was made into a movie. This event happened in the early thirties and all took place before I was born, but it is still talked about by the families today that live in the Missouri hills. I am sure there are still fox hunters back there, and it is my dream to someday return to those river and creek bottoms, and be able to hear the deep-throated guttural bawling, or the chopping voice of these dogs as they strike a hot trail. It is said that once a man's dream dies, he is soon to follow. I believe that owning a good dog and the thrill of hearing a long chase gave these men the courage and the will to fight their way through one of the most trying times our country has ever faced.

Chapter Twelve

Carl told Smitty all about the fox hunt and about seeing the ghost fox, he said, "We never got but just a glimpse of him, but it looked white all except his tail." Smitty was excited about the fox and wanted to go on a hunt, he asked Carl if he wanted to go with him and Grady some night. Dad told him he wouldn't get caught dead on a hunt with Grady. He said, "That greasy-haired bastard will catch on fire if he stands close to one. Hell, that Fitch's hair oil he bathes in is ninety percent alcohol."

Both men laughed and Carl told Smitty about some of the troubles he had with Grady.

He asked him what he was doing working for him. Carl just shook his head and said, "When it is the only show in town, that's the one you go to. If l could find another job I sure as hell wouldn't work for, or around that red-headed son-of-a-bitch." Smitty wanted to know more about Grady, but Carl figured he had said too much already so he went back to work.

Smitty really got chummy with Grady, it got to where he would ride with him around the work projects, even going fishing and hunting with him. He spent a lot of time with Grady over at the Judge's farm. Carl wondered if he was gathering evidence on the two men, or in corruption with them. He was very careful what he said to Smitty, no longer trusting the man.

It was October and just a few short weeks until the Christmas season, Dad didn't like Christmas much, but he did enjoy singing all the Christmas carols and the Christmas pageants that the school and church put on. It just seemed like he never had the money to buy his kids much. And soon he would have another one as Ruby was due anytime, this would make him nine kids. It seemed like all he had to do was look at Ruby and she would be pregnant again.

He loved all of his children, but the responsibility of providing for them was a heavy load.

On November the 9th nineteen and forty, Ruby gave birth to another girl; they named her Sally Juanita. She was a healthy baby with blond hair and deep blue eyes. Carl wondered about this as all the other kids had dark brown eyes, that come from the Indian blood in the family, but both Marvin and Evelyn had blond hair and blue eyes so he guessed it came from the Poolside of the family, which was of Dutch ancestry.

Ruby was totally exhausted after the birth, and the hernia that she suffered with the previous child was really hurting her. She was only able to stay up for short periods at a time.

This put more and more work on Vera, she was just fifteen and now had to do all the cooking and cleaning, her younger sister Jo Anna was thirteen and helped as much as she could, but Dad put it all on Vera. She had to get all the kids up in the mornings, make the beds, feed and dress the younger kids, plus make school lunches for her and five other children, and catch the bus by seven-thirty. One morning she missed the bus and Dad made her walk the three miles to Walnut Grove. She wanted to run away from home but our aunt Pauline talked her into staying, telling her that she only had one more year of school than she could go where ever she wanted.

Dad's back was bothering him more and more, he would take a door off of its hinges and lay it across two saw horses and with a blanket he would lie on it and try to sleep, hoping this would relieve some of the pain, some mornings he couldn't straighten up. It seemed to him on those days Grady gave him every hard lifting job he could find, or else he had to use a shovel all day, which irritated his back even more.

Ruby was really sick now and Vera was stuck with all of the housework. It was almost impossible for her to study. She would try and make everyone's lunch the night before so she would have more time in the mornings. Harve was only ten, but he did most of the milking, plus getting in all the wood and coal for heating and cooking.

Sally was just a little over two months old when Ruby realized that she was pregnant again. She was severally depressed; how would she ever manage ten children with four of them less than six years old? Dad was really angry when he found out, he even accused Ruby of messing around on him, she asked him when in the blue blazes of hell would she ever have time to run around. Telling him it was time he took responsibility for some of the children he was fathering. This caused him to go into a cussing fit as he stormed out the door.

It seemed like Carl was mad all the time now, he got up cussing and went to bed the same way. Ruby was so sick she stayed in bed as much as she could. She had six kids in school and three at home to watch when the older girls were gone. Don got to where he stayed over at Granddad's most of the time. They had cared for him so much when he was sick that he just took their place for home. They lived close by so he was always home during the time he wasn't in school, but he spent most of his nights at our grandparent's. He would get mad at Ruby when she had to discipline him, saying that she favored Marvin over him. So, he would head for Granddad's and stay a few days. Soon school was out for the summer, it seemed like kids were everywhere. We had moved to the rock house that used to belong to the preacher. It was made from marble stone that had been mined in the quarry across the road. There was a long sidewalk made from slabs of marble that ran almost to the little schoolhouse. All the kids rode bikes, skated and played games along in front of our house.

One fall day Marvin and Don, plus the Tuck boy never came home from school.

Harve went looking for them and they couldn't be found anywhere. Dad got home from work and they still were nowhere to be found. He walked over to Granddad's and they hadn't seen them, it was getting nearly dark when Granddad, Dad, and Mr. Tuck went looking for them. They searched the creek banks and up around the old Quarry. Dad even walked as far down to where the creek ran into the river. No one had seen the boys.

Shortly after dark, they came home each of them dragging a Christmas tree. The only thing wrong was it was in October, the boys were proud of the trees they had cut until their fathers got done spanking them, then they realized that Christmas was still a couple of months away.

As Don used to say, "Dad shouldn't have whipped us", as those were really nice Christmas trees and we had to walk nearly ten miles to find them. Granddad got a big laugh out of the whole thing; he was always telling the boys to go get another Christmas tree every time he saw them.

Dad had a rough time with all of his kids and their friends hanging around. They used to roll old automobile tires around the country, one day Dad was milking and he told the kids to go roll their tires someplace else, as they were scaring the cows. One of the boys rolled his tire and gave it a big kick. It took off across the yard, hit a tree, and changed directions, going straight for the barn. It ran into the cow Dad was milking; she jumped, kicked Dad, and the milk bucket fell over. He got up took off his belt and whipped every kid he could find, even a couple of the neighbor kids, going into the house he whipped my sister Jo Anna who was doing the dishes and didn't have any idea what the whipping was for.

I guess this made him feel better, things were pretty quiet for a while and he milked the old cows in peace.

Somehow the door to the feed room was left open, and our milk cow got into the feed, she ate until she was about to burst. By the time anyone figured out what had happened she was down and dying. This was a big loss to the family as the cow not only supplied milk, but butter and homemade cheese. Dad being very superstitious blamed the whole thing on the fact that someone had given him a two-dollar bill.

He ranted and raved saying, "I knew better than keep that damn bill, this is what I get for being so damn stupid." Giving the two-dollar bill to my brother, he had him go to the country store and buy a loaf of bread. The store owner wouldn't take it, telling my brother he would just put the price of the bread on my dad's grocery bill.

Dad was really in lather by now he threatened to bum the dang thing, but he didn't want to lose the two dollars, now that would really be bad luck. He walked over to uncle Joe's and he told him to just tear a comer off of the bill, that it would no longer be a whole two-dollar bill; therefore, it couldn't be bad luck anymore. Carl wasn't sure as he tore off a small comer, being sure not to damage the bill enough to lessen its value.

After he came home, he was still scared of the two-dollar bills and bad luck. Getting into the old Chevrolet he drove to Walnut Grove and got change for it. When he got home, he said if anyone ever gave him one of those damn things again, he was going to flatten their nose. That he ought to go back to the store in Springfield that gave it to him and make them pay for the cow. Ruby tried to reason with him about the two-dollar bill not having any more power over things than he gave it. This really sent Dad into a cussing fit. Finally, he said, "The damn things might not bring you bad luck. But why take the chance?"

For years I used to believe that they were bad luck. Looking back, I can see that there were a lot of superstitions among the hill folks. Like if a cow gave bloody milk, it was because someone in the family had killed a toad frog. The fact that one of the boys had run her for over a mile didn't have anything to do with it. I used to wonder how the dead frog knew which cow to put the curse on. No one ever went on down the road if a black cat crossed in front of them, they would always take another way around or wait until someone else came past, which in those days could take a long time. If a bird got into the house, someone in the family was surely going to die. People would worry for days after a bird had flown into their homes. You never stepped on a crack in the sidewalk, for to do so was going to cause serious injury to a loved one.

If a dog howled it meant that someone had just died. And forget walking under a ladder. This was sure to bring as much bad luck as breaking a mirror, which was good for seven years of misery to you. And don't pee in the middle of the road, for this will make a sty grow on your eye. If you curse on Sunday, it will make the milk turn blinky.

Granddad used to say he didn't curse when he got mad on a Sunday, but where he spit nothing would grow for the next five years.

If an owl hooted three times in succession it was sure to rain before morning. If a turtle bit you, he wouldn't turn loose until it thundered. And a dead snake wouldn't quit moving until after dark, even if you cut its head off. It was a mortal sin to open an umbrella inside the house, to do so would plague you with years of bad luck. And never kill a mockingbird if someone in the family was pregnant, to do so would cause the child to be born deaf and dumb. I am sure there are hundreds more but, these are some of the superstitions that I grew up with.

Thanksgiving Day 1941, All of Dad's brothers and sisters and their families were at Granddad's for dinner, the weather turned off cold and light snow was falling by the afternoon. Most of the men went hunting shortly after dinner and by the time they returned, the snow had turned to a freezing rain. As the day wore on the storm increased to the point most everyone headed for home. It wasn't long until Joe and his family came walking back down the road. He said, his car wouldn't go up Batson Hill, due to the ice and he was stuck in between the two hills.

Uncle Virgie went home and got his team of horses, with the men pushing, and the team pulling they managed to get the car back to the top of the first hill. By now the ice was over a half-inch thick on everything. Joe was afraid to try and go home so he came to our house and spent the night. The next morning there was an inch of clear ice frozen over everything. Tree limbs were falling everywhere as they broke under the load.

Dad went out to milk and two of the cows were down and couldn't get up. It took him, Joe, and the three oldest boys most of the morning to break the ice around them enough so the cows could get their feet under them.

The ice kept building and soon it was too dangerous to even go outside. Ruby tried to make a trip to the outhouse and took a nasty fall. She was a rather large woman and being eight months pregnant didn't help the situation any, it took Joe, Carl, and a couple of the boys to get her up and back to the house. The roads were so bad they couldn't go to the doctor, so Dad and Joe walked over to Grandma's and helped her over to the house. She stayed and cared for Ruby until the ice storm, which lasted several days was over. Joe was able to drive home and they all went back to work clearing the roads of downed trees and limbs. What few power lines there were in the country were all down and the men had to be very cautious about working around them.

The winter was bitterly cold and one of the worse anyone had ever seen. The men had to build large fires to warm by, to keep their feet and hands from freezing. A lot of cattle were lost from falling on the ice and not being able to get back up. It was impossible to get feed to a lot of the stock. Ice had to be broken on the pounds and rivers every few hours just so the cattle could drink. People couldn't get to the store and many of them were running short on wood and coal, it was a toss-up who was suffering the most the cattle or the people who tried to feed them.

Chapter Thirteen

The ice storm of November lasted into early December with many people being injured trying to do their daily chores and get to their jobs. On the morning of December the seventh 1941, I was only three and half years old, but I can still remember very clearly our neighbor Mrs. Fisher coming to our house early, she was in tears and very shaken.

She told my mother that the Japanese had bombed Pearl Harbor, Hawaii, and that her son Paul was over there.

Even though my Mother was about to give birth we all walked about a half mile to the neighbors who had a radio and listened to Mr. Roosevelt's speech where he declared war on the Japanese. My Mother and Mrs. Fisher were both in tears as we walked home, Mom held my hand tightly as Mrs. Fisher carried my sister Sally.

I can still picture the two women sitting at our table and discussing the fear of us going to war. Even as a small child, I could feel the fear they showed. Dad and Grandpa soon came home from work, everyone had been sent home early to be with their family while they waited for word from the government about what to do.

Many people gathered at the old Keel Hall, the minister let everyone in prayer for our servicemen and for the nation. No one really knew what to do so most just gather into small groups, and talked about what they expected to happen. Someone brought a radio in and everyone got quiet while they sat and listened to the news stories about the bombing and all the death and destruction. All of our battleships had been bombed and were on fire, many had sunk and the japs were still bombing. People were warned to be prepared for an invasion from within the country.

There were no Japanese living in the hills around Phenix, but there were some in Springfield. They were all immediately suspected of being spies. Many of the women returned to their homes and prepared food, which they brought to the hall. Soon the crowd grew really large as everyone listen to the news. Coffee and sassafras tea was made, as more and more food was brought in. Church services were held in the hall. People sang and prayed through the day, stopping every time there was a news flash on the radio.

Gradually everyone returned to their homes and farms. Young men plowed their fields wondering if they would still be around long enough for them to get planted. Any man between the ages of eighteen and thirty-six was required to register at the nearest postal facility. So many of the men were trying to enlist that the induction centers had to turn them away, being unable to handle the flood of people showing up. Each morning long lines could be seen forming around all of the enlistment centers.

Dad had just turned thirty-six, they wouldn't take him due to the number of children he had and with his blind eye made him ineligible. He said he could shoot and out-fight half of the people they were taking. Uncle Joe was only thirty but he had a heart murmur and was rejected. They both said they would rather fight japs than work for that damn Grady.

Word was spread that the judge had been arrested and was under investigation for taking kickbacks from the WPA workers, and for misuse of government funds. His bank had been closed and he was made to pay back all of the depositors. No one we knew had any money in the bank so it didn't faze anyone in our family.

The War news took presence over the judge being arrested, I guess it wasn't any surprise to most of the family that it happened, everyone knew that eventually, he would overstep the boundaries that he had been pushing on people. As the investigation into his dealing continued, many people were getting their children back from the orphanage.

Little was said about this as the radio only carried the war news and there wasn't anyone around that took a paper, most could hardly read one if they did.

###############

On December the 19th 1941 Ruby gave birth to another girl, they named her Barbra Kay, after Ruby's mother Barbra Pool. Kay had black hair and black eyes, unlike her blond blue eyed sister Sally. We were a mixed-up lot. The older sisters had red hair like all the Bradys from my father's mother's side of the family, Don and Marvin plus little sister Sally were blond blue eyes from the Pool side of the family, which were of Dutch ancestry. The rest of us had the dark features of the Indian blood from Granddad Keens side of the family.

Ruby now had two kids under a year old, Sally was only eleven months, I was three and a half, and Nancy was five. She spends every day scrubbing diapers on a washboard sitting in a tub of hot water that she had to pump and heat on a wood stove. The diapers would be hung outside in the cold where they would freeze dry. Vera and Jo Anna had to do most of the cooking and house cleaning. When Dad wasn't at work, he was with his father cutting firewood.

The winter of 41 and 42 was cold and long. All the young men were going off to war, and a lot of people were moving into the cities to work on the war machinery. Jobs were getting plentiful, as there was a shortage of able-bodied men. Many women were doing welding and mechanic work. The shipyards were now about sixty percent women workers. Dad, Joe and Granddad stayed with the WPA job.

Grady had really gotten nervous since the judge had been arrested; he tried to buddy up with everyone he had bullied, even trying to butter up to Carl, who wasn't having anything to do with him. Smitty had just disappeared one morning not saying a word to anyone. This really had Grady worried. Most of the road work was now being contracted out, or given to the county to complete. The WPA crews were almost all gone, there was just a few men left to clean up and finish some of the bridge work.

Joe had quit and was working for one of the road contractors. Word came down that a date had been set for the Judge's trial. And that the WPA projects would all be ended in six months due to the number of jobs being offered to people in the defense plants. Dad had applied for, and gotten a job at the Oreille Veteran's Hospital in Springfield. It was expanding its holding capacity due to all the wounded men being sent back from the war.

Granddad stayed on with the WPA until it ended then went back to farming and doing odd jobs around the area. There was a shortage of men in the community, so he was kept busy repairing homes and machinery.

Two days before the Judge's trial he was found shot to death sitting at his desk, there was reported to be over a hundred thousand dollars missing from his safe which was standing open. Everyone in the community was discussing who they thought had killed the judge, but his death has eventually declared a suicide.

The next day Grady didn't show up for work, and no one had seen him, his wife said he left during the night and hadn't returned. Weeks went by and still, there was no word about Grady or the missing money. He had just disappeared without any word, there was a lot of talk around the community, about how he probably faked the judge's suicide and stole the money. People started to lock their doors at night and look around more as they went about their chores. The daily war news soon took over, as the judge's death and the disappearance of Grady slowly drifted from people's minds.

Vera graduated from high school the spring of 1942. She moved to Springfield and entered nursing school. Jo Anna also moved to Springfield and stayed with our aunt Joyce my mom's sister, while she went to school and worked evenings. This really put a workload on Ruby, as Evelyn the oldest girl was only nine, and older brother Harve was thirteen. Brother Don now lived with our grandparents, leaving seven children still at home, four of them six or younger.

As the war went on, we had to black out the windows at night, but with only kerosene lamps that wasn't a big deal. Food was rationed and we had to have ration stamps to buy meat, sugar, coffee and other items, however there were enough kids in our family that we never went without. Dad would trade stamps with his brothers and other family members.

Coffee wasn't a big problem as most of the people drank sassafras tea, I can remember Dad and I fishing where Phenix Creek runs into Clear Creek, a large stand of sassafras brush was growing along the bank. It looked like someone had dug a lot of roots, as there was fresh dirt scattered everywhere. Dad told me to never dig the roots from these bushes because they weren't any good, that they were full of ants, and would taste bitter from the burdock that grew near them. (I still believe that Grady is buried there.)

Dad always had several fish traps set in the river, made from barrel hoops and chicken wire. We always seemed to have plenty of fish and every now and then we would get a large turtle. Granddad would boil the turtles in a large pot and strip the meat from them. I always preferred the white-looking meat as the dark tasted fishy to me. We couldn't get much fresh meat due to the war, so we ate a lot of wild game. Dad always butchered a few hogs every year. He and Granddad would kill wild rabbits, strip the meat from them and mix it with the pork and make sausage. We ate a lot of squirrels and woodchucks along with a few young raccoons.

We seemed to live well after the war started; Dad had a good job and was able to buy a car, along with other items for the house. He bought Mom a gas-powered washing machine that had wringers on it that would mash the water out of the clothes, making them easier to dry. Mom was always afraid one of the kids would get their hands caught in the wringers, so she wouldn't let any of us help feed the clothes into it. (I have heard of women getting other things caught in them.)

Things seemed to be going well for the Keen families, none of the boys had been injured in the war, and everyone that wanted a job could find one. Dad seemed happy all the time now he whistled or sang everywhere he went. I guess he was too happy as Ruby soon found that she was pregnant again. Even this didn't seem to bother him; he just said the more the merrier and took it all in stride.

On August 12, 1943, another girl was born into the family. They named her Phyllis Jean.

We had moved up toward the school into a house that was covered with marble rock from the quarry, it was known as the preacher's house. It had four rooms upstairs and a full basement. We had water here but we weren't supposed to use it. Mom always used it when she washed clothes. The basement always had tarantula spiders in it. Mom was deathly afraid of them and had all the kids scared of them also. I can remember her doing battle with one several times using a broom to chase it, they could jump several feet.

All of the old cellars around town had tarantulas in them, so we were afraid to play in those places. There was a small stream a short distance from our house, all of my brothers and sisters, plus a few dozen cousins dammed it up with large rocks, dirt, logs and anything else we could find. Soon we had a good swimming hole that was about six feet deep and twenty or thirty yards long.

Mom would always let us go play in the creek as she knew it wasn't but a few inches deep. One day she came down and seen the huge swimming hole, she was very upset but by then all of us had learned to swim, we had to show her that we could, so she let us go swimming as long as some of the older kids were with us. She and Dad often joined us in a good evening swim. It was a good place to play until a summer storm flooded the creek and our swimming hole washed full of gravel and the high water took out our dam. We tried to build it back, but it just never was the same again. There was a swinging bridge across the creek, it was two steel cables stretched about three feet apart, with four-foot planks bolted to it. The older boys could really get it to swinging and we really had to hold on to keep from falling the ten or so feet down to the creek. Mom being a large woman would never walk across it. She would always take her shoes off and wade across the creek. One day she slipped on a rock and fell throwing a spray of water clear up over the bridge, we all had a good laugh after we found out Mom wasn't hurt.

The little creek would dry up during the hot summer months leaving just small pools. The creek had a lot of large flat rocks in it. The water snakes would get under these to cool off. I had two dogs, a large collie that looked like Lassie and a small fox terrier. The two dogs and I would go snake hunting, I would lift up the rocks and snakes would go every direction, often between my feet. The dogs would grab them and sling their heads back and forth until they killed the snakes.

Sometimes one of the dogs would get bitten; they would lay around a few days with a large knot on their heads, as soon as they were feeling good we would go back to killing snakes again. I never got bit but had a lot of close calls. I started to school that August of 1943, even though I had just turned five in May. The little one-room schoolhouse in Phenix taught all eight grades in one room. We were seated in rows, with the first and second grades in the first two rows. And the other classes scattered out until the eighth-grade class set in the back of the room. My teacher was Mrs. Betty Daniels; she was a distant cousin on my Dad's side of the family. On my first day of school, I drew a picture of a cow with big udders on her, the teacher took a dislike to my drawing and when she let the class out for recess, she made me stay in the schoolhouse. She pulled my pants down and beat my bare butt with a wooden paddle that she kept hanging on her desk.

After she beat my butt, she ran her hands over my bare bottom and told me what smooth skin I had. I didn't realize it then but I think this teacher had a problem. My sister heard me getting the spanking and run home to tell Mom. We lived only a half block from the school. Even though Mom had three small children that weren't school age she quit what she was doing and walked over to the school. After confronting Mrs. Daniels, she took her by the hand and walked her over to where the cows were and they had a discussion about the tits on a cow and the art work of a five-year-old boy. I never was Mrs. Betty's favorite student after that, but she left me alone for a few months, I think she was scared of my Mother.

Chapter Fourteen

School wasn't much fun after I got my butt beat, I was afraid of my teacher and being the youngest boy in school it seemed like I was always getting into trouble of some kind. One day at recess the older boys chased a flying squirrel up a large hickory tree, they threw rocks at it until the little squirrel spread it sides and sprang from the tree. As it sailed down toward the ground, I was going to be the hero so I caught it in midair. I didn't hold onto it very long; just enough for it to bite me through several fingers on each hand. Really it didn't take me that long to look at the squirrel.

My older brothers scolded me for being so dumb, and the teacher yelled at me as she poured that dang burning iodine all over my cuts while I stood crying and dancing. My hands were so sore I couldn't hold a pencil right for several weeks. I had a cousin that was in the same grade as I was and I really didn't like her. She was always running and telling on everyone. One day an older boy talked me into sticking a stick through a knot hole in the girl's toilet and goosing her with it as she sat down. She let out a blood-curdling scream and went running and crying to the teacher.

For the second time in not so many weeks I got detained at recess, and again my pants were pulled down and I was forced to lean over the teacher's desk as she applied that damn paddle to my bare butt with several swift strokes. This time she didn't rub my sore butt; she just shook me real good, gave me a lecture and told me to go tell my Mother what I had done. I went back to the playground and begged my sister not to tell on me. But old big mouth couldn't get home fast enough to spill the beans. Mom asked me why I did it and I told her that Don told me to. Ruby, being the kind understanding mother that she was gave me two more spankings, one for me and one for Don.

I was beginning to hate school, especially now that it was springtime and the sun was out. I would sit in the schoolroom and think about all the crawfish, small perch, and snakes that my dogs and me could chase along the creek. The teacher was always hollering at me to pay attention. (I suppose if that happened now, they would dope me up on Riddling, and say I had attention deficit disorder.)

The teacher kept that big wooden paddle with the four holes drilled in it hanging on the front of her desk. I hated that thing as I sit in the front seat close to it. I had to look at that instrument of torture every day, and I knew how it felt on a bare butt, as did several of the other boys. One day we had a substitute teacher and my brother Marvin stole the paddle; all of us scratched our names on it and threw it into the creek that ran past the school. We stood and threw rocks at that demon thing until it floated out of site on down the creek.

Not a word was ever mentioned about it being gone. I would sit and look at the empty nail and smile to myself, knowing that instrument of torture would never beat my butt again.

There was a large spring that ran out of the hillside just below the school, someone had built a cement wall around it making a pool of water about four feet square and a couple of feet deep. Some of the kids would bring a jar of milk to drink with their lunch. They would put it in the spring setting it on a large rock just under the water to keep it cold. I caught a large crawfish one day and put it in my cousin's jar of milk. We were sitting in the classroom eating our lunch when she took a big drink. The crawfish not liking the milk bath grabbed hold of her lip; she let out a scream and spit milk all over books, desk and everyone around including the teacher. Her jar of milk flew across the floor further than she flung the crawfish.

Everyone in the room thought she had gone mad as she was standing dancing in a pool of milk and screaming as loud as she could. I was choking on my lunch from laughing so hard. Even my two brothers looked scared as all the girls were climbing upon their desks trying to escape from the horrible whiskered creature with the big claws that was scurrying backward across the milk-soaked floor.

Mrs. Betty finally got everyone settled down as one of the boys caught the crawfish and returned him to the creek from whence he came. Not even asking who did this horrible thing, she immediately got me by the arm, led me to the front of the room, reached into a desk drawer and brought forth a new paddle that was made from shiny wood. I can still remember the sight of it, there were only three holes drilled into this one. I could tell that it had never been used. I should have felt honored being I was to be the first to receive its stinging force.

Mrs. Betty never bothered to drop my drawers; I guess she didn't want to embarrass me in front of the whole school. She just bent me over the front of her desk and commenced to beat the living daylights out of an innocent child. I must say the new paddle worked as well as the old one. And of course, my big-mouthed sisters had to run home and blab everything to mom; she didn't even wait for school to be out.

I tried to blame everything on one of my brothers or anyone else that might have done it. I can say this I got the whipping for it but they never did make me confess. I even lied to Mom telling her I was afraid of crawfish. I know the teacher always thought I was the guilty party but she never knew for sure. I could always tell that she had doubts whenever she looked at me.

I made it through the first grade with only three spankings at school. Not a bad record for a little five-year-old boy who never meant anyone any harm. (Well maybe a little to my cousin Carole Sue) who I learned to love dearly after we got older.

Summer flew by like it does in the years of our youth, I spent most of it playing along the creek and going fishing with my brothers and cousins. The war was taking a toll on the community as several of the boys had been killed or badly wounded. When there was a military funeral at the small Greene Lawn cemetery, which was just a mile or so up the road. We would walk up and watch the processions and jump when the guns were fired in honor of the dead. The haunting sound of taps being played still makes me cry whenever I hear it. The only other sound that ever stirred me as much is the Indian death chant played on a lone drum and chanted by a solitary person from a far-off distance.

I was always amazed by the colors of the shoulder patches the different military men wore. One of them gave me a small flag and a patch that had a white star on it with gold wings circled by red and a black border. Mom sewed these onto a blue shirt of mine; I wore this shirt with pride saving the flag and patch long after the shirt was worn out.

Even as a small child, I could see the pride the soldiers and sailors had in wearing our country's uniforms.

It was now fall and as we showed up for a new school year that morning and took our places in the school room, there hanging on the nail in front of Mrs. Daniels desk was that ugly old four-hole paddle, it was weather-worn and bleached by the sun. Someone had taken a lead pencil and boldly traced over each name that had been scratched into the wood. I could read my name from where I sat; man I wished I hadn't scratched it in such large letters.

It stuck out so much more than any of the others. I think whoever did this, did it just to cause me pain and suffering. I wanted to get up and run from that place and never come back again. As Mrs. Daniels came in and greeted us all with a good morning and a welcome back, I tried to slink down behind my desk. I never once made eye contact with her.

Being the lady she was, she never mentioned the paddle. She didn't have too, nor did she have to use it at all that year. It just hung there threatening each and every one of us that had scribed our names on it. A gray bleached piece of wood about sixteen inches long with four holes evenly spaced down the center and a neatly carved and worn handle. This instrument of pain and suffering should be in the archives along with the rack and guillotine. A hunk of driftwood that Mrs. Betty had found in a large drift along the creek that flows through her property, its very existence took a lot of mischievous thought out of the minds of many a young boy.

I can't remember much about my second grade; I do remember the war news and everyone who could buy savings stamps. A stamp cost a dime and was kept in a book until they were worth enough to trade for a savings bond. Some of the wealthy kids would buy a dollar's worth of them at a time. We could never afford even one measly stamp.

This always embarrassed all of us who were so poor. I do remember one time a cousin of mine bought ten dollars' worth and he let me help him glue them into his book. I had never seen so many savings stamps in my life.

I would always walk across this large field when I went home from school, my little fox terrier dog would come and meet me. I carried my lunch to school in a shiny syrup bucked that had a nice snap lid on it. One day a woodchuck came out of its burrow and my little dog attacked it. The woodchuck had my dog by the lip and he was howling and yelping very loud, I ran up and started beating it with my lunch pain until it released my dog. When I got home, I had to explain to dad how my lunch pail got so beat up, when I told him the story, he scolded me and said I was lucky I didn't get bit. My lunch bucket was bent and battered, but we had won the fight and I carried that pail with pride for several years.

Back during the war years all of the older boys bought their shotguns and rifles to school, and would hunt rabbits and squirrels on the way home. My brothers would set box traps along the fence rows to catch rabbits, one evening after school I noticed one of the traps was sprung. Tipping the trap up I slowly raised the lid and sure enough there was Mr. Rabbit, laying my books and lunch pail down I reached in and got him by the ears like I had seen my brothers do, only thing I didn't grab the back feet so as I pulled him from the trap, he raked me across the belly with his sharp claws tearing my shirt and ripping open my skin. Me being the sharp alert boy I was, I immediately released Mr. Rabbit and took concern with my bleeding stomach, and torn shirt.

When I got home mom was very upset with me, as were my brothers, I had turned loose dinner and gotten scratched up for my troubles. Everyone seemed to be more concerned about the loss of the dang rabbit, than they were about my injuries. When Dad came home, he gave me a lecture about the danger I had put myself in, and he immediately told the older boys to show me how to take a rabbit out of a trap, and kill it without getting scratched. Several days later I came by another trap that was sprung, now I really had my nerve up and I was going to show the world that I was big enough to take a rabbit from a trap, and kill it. I tipped the box trap up and opened the lid without looking inside. I reached my hand in to get the rabbit by the ears, when a yellow cloud of stinking stuff come flying out of the trap hitting me on the arm, face, and in one eye.

I was in total shock as I rocked back letting the trap fall to the ground, I stood there retching and gasping for air as a black and white animal walked from the trap and let me have another shot, this time hitting me squarely in both eyes. I couldn't see and I couldn't breathe as I ran stumbling falling and crying for home. Mom heard me screaming and come running, suddenly she stopped holding her hand out as to push me away, she said don't come any closer. Here I was in severe pain and agony, and the one person I thought would bring me comfort wouldn't let me get close to her.

My big-mouth snotty-nosed sisters all line up holding their noses and laughed at me, while my two brothers stood there with a smirk on their faces. Mom told them to get a wash tub and fill it with water; she made me take off all my clothes right there in front of everyone. My faithful little dog come running up to me, took one sniff and high-tailed it to the barn as if I had kicked him in the butt.

I stood there bare ass naked as my brothers filled a tub with cold well water. Mom made me sit in this ice-cold mess why she gagged and scrubbed the skin off of me with a bar of lye soap. She wrapped an old towel around me and made me sit outside in the wind for over an hour. Picking up my clothes with a stick she draped them over the lilac bush. Of course, every neighbor girl in town had to come over about that time, they all stood with my sisters pointing fingers at me, and laughing like I was the number one freak show in town. Dad tried to talk to me about my little episode without laughing, explaining that other animals get into box traps besides rabbits, as if I didn't know.

Everyone in the family called me stinky for several months, and the kids at school would hold their noses and run whenever I got near them.

My uncle Joe took me fishing one day and told me about the time he got sprayed by a skunk, after that I didn't take it so personal. It just seemed like every bad thing that could happen, always happened to me.

Chapter Fifteen

I learned quickly from the episode with the skunk, how to look into a box trap very carefully, and to take a rabbit from a trap without getting scratched. My older brothers would go coon hunting at night with the dogs. I would cry and beg to go; sometimes they would take me along even though they didn't want to. I was really scared of the dark and being out in the woods made it worse. My brothers would turn off the lantern and holler, "What's that?" Then they would run in every direction and hide, leaving me standing alone in the dark screaming and crying. They would pull limbs back and let them smack me in the face as we walked along. If I threatened to tell Dad they said they wouldn't let me come along anymore.

I soon grew tired of their game so one night I got a flashlight and hid it in my coat. We were off in the woods when they played their running game. I let out a loud cry then sneaked off and hid in some bushes. I must have been hid for close to a half hour. I could see them lighting the lantern, they started hollering for me. I set there ever so quiet snickering to myself as they hunted and hollered for me.

Soon they really became concerned about my whereabouts, I never moved as they started whistling and hollering for me. I could hear them cussing and saying they were going to leave me out there. After they had walked off a way I snuck out of my hiding place and went home. They stayed in the woods most of the night searching, afraid to come home without me. When they finally did come home and found me in bed asleep, they were so angry that they woke Dad up and wanted him to give me a whipping. As I can remember, this was the last time I ever went hunting with my brothers at night.

My Dad would take me squirrel hunting with him, our little fox terriers would bark at the trees and we would walk around it several times trying to find the squirrel. It was a contest between Dad and me to see who could spot that busy tail blowing in the breeze first. There were a lot of squirrels in the hickory and walnut forest that grew along the rivers, and during the spring time they especially loved to eat the maple seeds that grew in the whirly pods that fall from the trees.

We would sit real still and Dad would get two rocks and hit them together making a scraping sound that imitated a squirrel's chatter. It wouldn't take long for one to answer him. Calling them in close, he would only shoot the young ones, because the old squirrels were too tough to eat. I got to shoot the rifle quite a bit and was able to hit a target most the time. One day a squirrel came into a tree close to us and Dad let me shoot it. I held the gun real tight and never breathed as I took careful aim and pulled the trigger, as the rifle cracked the squirrel jumped and fell from the limb. I ran over and picked it up. Then it hit me, I had killed a living thing. As I looked into the dead black eyes of the little squirrel, I wanted it to come back alive and run from us.

I had never given any thought to killing things before, they were always killed for food or because they were doing damage to something. I sat there beside my father looking at the poor lifeless creature that I had just shot. It wouldn't quit looking at me with those little black beady eyes, slowly I reached over and run my hand thought the soft fur and stroked the fluffy tail as a lump formed in my throat. A sharp crack from the rifle brought me back to reality, Dad had shot another Squirrel. I ran out and picked it up as it fell from the tree. We have enough for a good supper he said, going over to a little spring I watched him skin the squirrels, wash the meat and put it in a bread wrapper he carried in his pocket.

I guess I had turned into a hardened killer, for it never bothered me to shoot a rabbit or squirrel after that. It was just all part of life and the necessity to survive. It must be part of my Indian heritage, as my father and grandfather were both excellent shots and good hunters. It has always been in my blood to hunt, even when I don't need the meat there is a call to the outdoors that lurks deep in my soul. But with that comes a need to conserve, I have been called a packrat by some of my friends and family.

Growing up during the war years we never wasted anything and pretty much lived off the land, there were always fish traps set in the river, and animal traps set around the countryside. The meat was eaten, the pelts cleaned and sold for fur. There wasn't any deer, and most of the wild hogs had been killed off, so it was all small game. The feathers from ducks and geese were washed and used to stuff pillows or feather ticks.

We drank lots of tea made from the sassafras roots, and collected hickory nuts and black walnuts. We picked wild cherries, possum grapes, persimmons, and lots of wild blackberries were canned. These were heated up and served in a bowl with hot biscuits for breakfast. We raised hundreds of pounds of potatoes and sweet potatoes that were stored in the root cellars along with pumpkins and squash. There were bins of apples and pears. It was my job every Saturday to go through them and throw out any rotten fruit or potatoes. The smokehouse always had smoked hams, and sides of smoked bacon hanging in it. We might have been dirt poor but no one ever went hungry.

Mom worked from early morning until late at night, trying to keep all of us fed and clothed. We might not have worn the latest fashions, but our clothes were always clean and well-mended.

I recall one morning I had started to school and discovered a large hole in the crotch of my pants, I turned around and headed back to the house. There were several kids from school passing by and I didn't want them to know why I went back. Mom met me on the sidewalk and told me to get to school. It was springtime and she had caught me skipping school several times and playing all day along the creek. I told her I needed to go into the house but she wouldn't let me tell me again to go to school.

I wasn't about to mention my ripped britches to her right in front of all those girls, especially as it was in the center of the crotch. Mom broke off a switch and began to whip me right there in front of everyone. I stood there very defiantly and took the whipping; finally, she got me by the arm and marched me into the house where she kept the belt. I told her my pants were ripped and I needed to change.

She was very upset and asked me why I didn't tell her that; I told her I didn't want the other kids to know I had a hole in the crotch of my pants, especially the girls. Mom told me she was sorry for whipping me in front of everyone, I changed clothes and run to school. Only was a few minutes late, but late enough that the teacher made me stand in the corner for fifteen minutes. I hated that dang teacher and she hated me, school was like a prison in the springtime.

I could look out of the windows and see the sun shining, flowers blooming and birds building nests. I never learned a thing that time of year; my mind was always someplace else. I got scolded a lot for daydreaming, as the teacher called it. I had some words for her too, but I kept them to myself.

There was a special secluded place I had that was on a big rock bluff overlooking the creek; it was shaded by two big paw-paw trees, whose large limbs hung down over the rock and along each side completely hiding it. I believed I was the only person in the whole wide world that knew of this place. When I wanted to be alone, I would sneak along through the weeds and between the branches making sure no one has seen me. I spent many hours here on this rock with my dog, just watching the clouds float by, and listening to the gurgling sound of the little stream that ran past.

One morning a man from the marble company came by the house and told Mom that we had to move. The company was closing down everything it owned. There were just a few houses left in the Phenix vicinity, granddad and grandmother had moved out to the farm north of Walnut Grove. Most of the Bradys and a lot of the Keens had moved to Springfield or went on to California.

Dad rented a three-bedroom house in Walnut Grove, a place known as the old Cantrell house. It had been built many years before by Dr. Cantrell who was a dentist and a medical doctor combined. The place was very primitive with no indoor plumbing and only one electric light in each room, which hung down on a long cord and had a pull chain to turn it off and on. There weren't any cabinets in the kitchen, just a big wood cook stove. The floors were very uneven as the house had settled so bad that none of the interior doors would shut.

I can't remember what time of year it was when we moved, I just remember the two dogs jumping into the car with the last load without anyone calling them. School had started so I was the new kid in my grade; I believe it was my third year in school. My new teacher's name was Mrs. Hagerman, she was an older lady but very friendly. Of course, being the new kid, I had to go through the pecking order with most of the boys. I got into a shoving match with a bigger kid during the first recess. At lunch, he walked by and pushed me again. I gave him a bloody nose and had to stand in the comer for the rest of the day. He must have been the leader as all the other boys left me alone, after that. I thought I was tough, but I found out later it was because my two older brothers told everyone not to bother me.

The city school was quite a change from the little one-room school in Phenix. It was a two-story building with a full gymnasium in the basement. There were eight rooms on the first floor and four on the top, plus a large study hall and auditorium. The auditorium was above the gym, when they had a program there all of us poor kids had to set in the gym, as we couldn't afford the cost of a nickel to watch the show. We were not permitted to play on the gym as it had a hardwood floor and any shoes would make marks on it.

Sometimes we could take our shoes off and play in our stocking feet, my socks had so many holes in them I wouldn't take my shoes off. We could hear the kids laughing and applauding as they watched the show. This cause me to have a bitter dislike for all of them. They would come around us and talk about everything they had seen, in order to make us jealous. I would listen for a while, until some smart ass would ask why I didn't go. I always said I had already spent my dollar allowance for the week, or that I was saving my money to buy a new rifle. Of course, I never got a nickel allowance let alone a dollar. But it shut them up. I soon developed a bitter dislike for people with money. They were always flashing it around, kids at school would have several pieces of change in their pockets, and they would pull it out and count it in front of all the poor kids. There was a candy bar machine at the school, these kids would buy a candy bar, eat half of it and throw the rest in the trash, and laugh as the poor kids fought to get it. I hated the snooty little bastards. I called them that to myself.

These kids always got picked to play the best parts in the school programs, and got the most attention from the teachers. All of this just made me hate them that much more I could never see why they were treated so much better than the rest of us. But now I realize it was because their fathers were on the school board.

They would always have a big box of crayons with thirty or forty colors in them, and a big chief tablet that was about a half-inch thick. We only could afford a penny tablet and a box of colors with maybe a dozen in it. I guess it was envy or jealousy but all this made me very angry. I would get in fights at recess and lunchtime with these kids, as they always had candy and cake in their lunch when all we ever had was a sandwich or a biscuit with a hunk of side meat, and a wormy apple.

When we played games, the rich kids would choose sides and all the poor kids would always be the last ones picked to play on their teams. I refused to be the last one picked so I would always get the poor kids to make up a team of our own, we all had to work milking cows and do chores, so we had a lot of muscle and were always tougher than most. If we were losing, I always got rough and tried to put some hurt on them. There was one big kid named Rodger that liked to push me down, trip me, or hit me. One day I picked up a rock and when he shoved me, I slapped him beside the head with it. Causing a pretty good wound on his head. He hit the ground screaming in pain, which scared me a little, he got up and run to the school house hollering for the teacher. Blood was running down his hand as he held onto his head. The rock had caused a pretty good cut on the side of his head just above the ear, and he was bleeding pretty well. The teacher was scared and hollering about what happened. "Rodger said he fell and hit his head on something." She grabbed a shirt someone had left in the classroom and held it to the cut. One of the other teachers volunteered to drive him to the doctor.

All the kids were gathered around looking scared, guess I did too, as I didn't mean to really hurt him that bad, but I owed him a good knot on his head, too bad he doesn't know I whacked him a good one on purpose. Really, I was glad no one saw it. Our teacher took all of us out to the playground and told us to look for anything that would hurt us if we fell. It didn't take me long to find the rock I whopped Rodger with. I picked it up and threw it over in the ditch by the road, thinking, man I am glad no one has seen all that I had done.

We had a boy in the third grade named Johnny that really had problems. His family was really poor, he didn't have shoes to wear in the summer and never had anything but overalls to wear that were too big for him. His father was always drunk and causing trouble with everyone. Jonny was what they now call dyslectic. He would always write all his letters backward. The teacher would write the letter S on the blackboard and have him stand there and copy it. He would always have it facing the wrong way, she would swat him with the paddle and tell him to make it right, he would stand crying and shaking and draw it wrong again. The teacher would paddle him and he would cry and shake until he would pee his pants. I remember crying when she did this, I felt so sorry for him.

Johnny quit coming to school a month or two after that. I would see him at the store sometime with his drunken father, he was always dirty ragged, and had a runny nose, he would say hello and then try to hide in another aisle. We were poor but nothing like his family. I doubt if his father ever worked a day in his life. I know his mother did laundry and house cleaning for some of the wealthy people in town.

The war changed lives for a lot of people, boys were killed and others come home missing arms or legs. My older brother was in the Navy and we got word that his ship was sunk and he was missing. Dad never ever gave up, he always said that boy is a survivor and he is ok someplace. We finally got word that he was in a hospital in New Caledonia and that he was ok. It wasn't long until the war was over and most of the men came home.

I made it ok in school for the next few years, had a boy named Larry that bullied me in the eighth grade, he was two years older than me but a grade behind me. I don't know why he didn't like me, only that his family had money he thought he was the king of the town. He gave me a black eye one evening after school and I ran from him. This never did stick well in my craw. My Uncle told me that the next time he got in my face to reach up and get hold of my ear, to strike him in the nose with the palm of my hand with a straight-out punch. He caught me in the boy's restroom shortly after that, Larry had his face right in mine so close his stinking breath was about to gage me, I was really scared as I reach up and got hold of my ear lobe real slow, and a straight-out punch with my hand open I got him square in the nose with the heel of my hand. His head flew back and blood flew everywhere, I hit him in the nose again with my fist, and ran from the room as fast as I could go. I was scared but felt proud of myself. After school, Larry was waiting for me with another boy. His nose was blue and swelled to twice its size. He told me that when his nose was healed up, he was going to give me the beating of my life. I thought what the hell, so I hit him again in his swelled-up nose, he hit the ground holding it with both hands as blood ran between his fingers, I was brave then, I asked the other kid if he wanted some of it and he left. Larry was crying and holding his face, I asked him if he had had enough, but he just walked off crying and bleeding.

That evening his father came to our farm and got onto my dad about the fight. My father wasn't one to fool with, he grabbed him by the front of his shirt with both hands and told him if Larry ever laid another hand on me, he would have one of the older boys whip his ass. That this had been going on too long and he never said anything about me coming home with black eyes, giving him a shove, Dad told him to get the hell off our farm, before this becomes a father and son project.

School was soon out for the summer, I had never seen Larry all summer and that fall when school started, I had grown a lot and filled out enough, that I was now as big as or bigger than Larry. I went out for football and we had practice every day after school so I never saw much of him. He always spoke to me when we passed in the hall, I never trusted him and was no longer scared. But I was always ready if he wanted trouble.

Dad had sold all the cows and took a job in Springfield working for Burge Hospital. Finally, I could sleep until six or seven after having to get up at 4:30 every morning. I set traps along the farm pounds and streams near our house all that winter. My brother Marvin milked cows for a neighbor woman. After he graduated high school, he was drafted and went into the Navy.

I took over the job milking cows for the widow woman, so never had time after school to get into trouble, with that job and the chores I had to do at home I was kept busy. During the summer months, I worked for a lot of the farmers putting up hay, I had a friend named Bobby that milked for me during that time. He was a big tall kid over six foot six and quite a basketball player.

I was only sixteen during my whole senior year, so I was playing football against boys that were a couple of years older than me. I held my own but was intimidated by some of the older boys. I never was a superstar like some of the players were, always wished I had had a couple of years more growth on me. I loved the game and still do. As I look back, I can see where I didn't really know what I was supposed to do, as I would block players on defense instead of getting to the ball carrier. We had a good team that could have been a lot better if we would have had more coaches and better equipment.

I never made it as a basketball player, I seemed to get into foul trouble pretty quick and I was always angry if I had to sit on the bench when I figured I was a lot better than some of the boys playing. A lot of it was who your daddy was, if you played or not. I never realized how much politics affected a small school. Wonder what it was like in a large school? Probably worse.

I tried to play college ball after I graduated but soon found out those boys play for keeps and really intimated this little country boy, who wasn't near as tough as he thought he was. I had never been in a weight room, so didn't have the large bulky muscles those athletes had. What muscles I had were hard but not bulky. I was faster than they were but should have been a couple of years older.

Chapter Sixteen

Growing up as a kid in Missouri was in itself a challenge. It seemed each day was a special event, but I was too young to realize just how much fun it was. I had three very special friends that all went by nicknames. There was Wheezer and Hoppy who were brothers and then there was Tooter who was a cousin.

Wheezer suffered from an asthma condition and when he breathed it sounded like the screeching of a rusty gate hinge. Hoppy always went barefooted like the rest of us, but for some reason, his feet were never calloused like ours. He always had a stubbed toe or stone bruise on one foot or the other. He was always walking on his heel which caused him to hop when he walked. Tooter takes a little more explaining, he always had gas, which was caused by his steady diet of beans and cabbage, causing him to toot with each step he took, or anytime he exerted himself. He would always laugh, which caused him to toot even more.

All three boys had the gaunt sunken eyes and high cheekbones of the undernourished children. There wasn't an ounce of fat on any of them. And their skin was baked brown from the summer sun. They called me big'en or just plain big, as I was taller and heavier than any of them. Our fathers were all share croppers and worked us in the fields when they could catch us. Most of the time we spent swimming and playing along the river.

One summer day in late August we had three coon hounds with us. They chased a raccoon out of a brier thicket and up into a hollow tree that leaned out over the river.

When Hoppy had two good feet, he could climb almost anything. On this day he was suffering from a stubbed toe that was swollen and very sore. He was hobbling along with a kerosene-soaked rag tied around it. One end of the rag had become untied and flopped in the air with each step he took.

We chased after the old coon with Wheezer sounding like a worn-out siren, Hoppy's sore toe rag flopped in the air with each step he took. Tooter was playing music with each step keeping us all at a distance. We could see a large hollow spot up in the tree as the hounds bayed and chewed at the tree trunk trying to climb it.

Hoppy forgot about the sore toe as he climbed up to the hollow spot. I can't see anything but get me a forked stick and I will twist him out.

We cut a green hickory sprout from a bush that was growing along the river bank. Trimming it up and leaving a short fork on the end of it. Hoppy began poking the stick into the hole saying, "I can feel him" as he poked and twisted the stick into what he thought was the old coon's fur.

After a few more pokes and twists, Hoppy began yelling ouch, ouch, letting out a scream as he came sliding down out of the tree with leaves, limbs, and bark falling all around him. When he hit the ground the rag on his sore toe flopped in the air, one old hound expecting a coon to come down grabbed hold of Hoppy's sore toe. He let out a loud scream, hollering get him off, get him off me. Tooter yanked on the dog's collar letting off a series of loud toots that simultaneously filled the air with a foul odor.

Wheezer became excited and started wheezing and screeching, as the hounds bayed and bawled. Tooter kept trying to get the dog off Hoppy, who was now on his back crying and holding his toe up to his mouth blowing on it. Every time he moved his foot the end of the oily rag flapped in the breeze and another hound would snap at it. Tooter let loose of a hound and a loud toot at the same time. Again, the hound latched onto Hoppy's toe. He screamed and hollered all the time kicking at the dog with his good foot.

Getting to his feet he smacked Tooter in the nose, knocking him back into Wheezer who by now was gasping and turning blue as his lungs sucked up all the dust and dirt caused by Hoppy's fight with the dogs.

About now I began to find out what was happening as the air became filled with angry honey bees. Hoppy had been poking the forked stick into a wild honey bee hive. Tooter got stung about the same time letting out a toot that sounded like a lonesome train whistle on a cold winter night. He stood there screaming, crying and tooting as blood trickled down his nose from the blow Hoppy had struck him.

A sting to the ear brought Wheezer back to reality causing him to suck in all the wind he could, causing a screeching sound deep in his chest. Hoppy was now cussing and swatting bees with both hands while running for the river with the sore toe rag still flopping in the breeze. The only dog that hadn't tasted the kerosene-soaked rag on Hoppy's toe decided to take a nip at what he thought was a coon's tail as it flashed by him.

Latching onto Hoppy's sore toe sent both of them flying end over end. Wheezer was trying to run, breathe and scream at the same time. Tooter ripped out another loud toot that kept the bees at bay around him. I passed them all up with a dozen bees in my curly hair stinging me. I dove head-first into the river and began splashing water on my head trying to rid myself of the bees. Hoppy came limping down to the water's edge, crying and cussing with blood running from his sore toe, the kerosene rag had gotten ripped off with the last dog bite. Wheezer came running by still swatting at bees and wheezing like an old steam tractor. He stepped on Hoppy's sore toe, which got him a fist in the eye. He let out a loud wild scream mixed with a long coughing wheeze, just as Tooter who was now holding a bloody nose with one hand and swatting bees with the other ran into him, and knocked him into the river.

Causing him to grab Hoppy and pull him in with them. I was still swatting bees as Wheezer gasp for air and got choked on the water, his face was turning blue and his brown eyes showed only the whites as they rolled back into his head. All the time Hoppy was trying to stand on one foot and look at his mangled toe. Tooter just stood out in deep water blowing bubbles from his backside while he wiped blood and snot from his nose.

Everyone was yelling, cussing and screaming. The hounds were barking and baying so loud that a farmer that was plowing a field nearby, came running down to the river to see if we were all right. He took one look at Wheezer and jumped into the river to save him. Tooter started laughing causing him to agitate the water even more. Wheezer seeing the old farmer coming at him run into deeper water trying to get away which caused him to breathe even harder or else try to, I don't think he was getting much air at the time.

Once he got near Tooter, he changed directions as the air over there wasn't too good.

I finally wore the bees out that were in my hair, and crawled out on the bank in time to help the farmer pull Wheezer out of the water.

By now Hoppy was mad and starting to cuss between whimpers as he looked at his mangled toe. Tooter came up the bank but we made him walk off downwind while the farmer tried to get some good air back into Wheezer's lungs at the same time asking us what was going on. The more we told him about our tale of woe, the harder he laughed, which caused Tooter to laugh and toot some more. Hoppy couldn't see anything funny about it as he cursed and blew on his toe. I set and rubbed the bee stings on my head as I watched Wheezer's blue complexion return to a somewhat normal color. We thanked the farmer, who was still laughing, for coming down and checking on us, he waved goodbye, as Tooter gave him a final salute. It was just another day in the life of a poor country boy.

Chapter Seventeen

On Thanksgiving Day 1949, my parents drove to Seymour Missouri to have Thanksgiving dinner with my mother's sister. Leaving the rest of us at home. Mom had fixed a large dinner for all of us. All we had to do was heat it up.

That afternoon the weather changed to a cold windy freezing rain with snow flurries. We gathered a lot of coal and wood for the fires made hot chocolate and got a board game going.

Soon it was past bedtime, so we all wandered off to bed, except for Evelyn and Nancy who stayed up to wait for the folks to get home. When it got daylight, they still hadn't gotten back. We figured that the roads had gotten slick and they had stayed all night somewhere. The girls fixed breakfast for the rest of us. My brothers and I milked the cow and took care of all the outdoor stuff. Getting the coal buckets filled up and wood in for the cook stove.

Later that morning my dad's brother Wilburn and his wife Anna came over and told us Mom and Dad had been in a bad car wreck and were in the hospital in Springfield. Both of them had been badly injured. It was several weeks before they could come home, Dad had a broken leg, and his skull and jaws had been fractured, he had wires running through the top of his head to hold his jaws in place, and he could only suck soup and stuff through a straw, his arms and hands had been badly cut and one wrist was broken. Mom had a fractured cheekbone a broken nose, a broken collar bone and a cracked pelvis. They both had to be helped to walk. Uncle Wilburn and Anna stayed and took care of us kids until the folks got home. I don't know what we would have done without their help. One of them was always there to help out for several weeks. I remember Uncle Wilbur was going to wash my face one morning and I run from him. I was eleven years old and pretty fast, but not fast enough, he caught me and busted my butt and really washed my face, I minded him real well after that. He was a good man and always treated me well. Taking me hunting and fishing a lot. I will always be grateful for the way him and my other uncles treated me.

There were a lot of hunting and fishing and camping trips I would have never gotten to go on, if not for them. When I played football there would always be a couple of my uncles watching. Sometimes telling me what I did wrong, and how I could play better. I tried to take their advice and most of the times it worked.

My uncle Joe would take me frogging, we would walk along the banks in the water and spot frogs setting on the bank. Blind them with a flashlight and grab them. We always carried a feed sack to put them in. It was a real race sometimes when we got too close to a snake and the water would part as we got away as fast as we could. We had a lot of fun kidding each other about who was the most afraid of snakes. All I know, I was the fastest but I never wanted to get in Joe's way.

Dad decided to raise turkeys one time, we had a long-slanted building. With several kerosene heaters to keep them, warm.

One morning I went out to check on the baby turkeys and found about a dozen of them dead, they had been bitten through the head and the blood sucked out. Dad said it must be a weasel as nothing else could get into the shed. He told me to take the old double barrel twelve-gauge shotgun and set out there and kill whatever there was that was killing the turkeys.

Now at twelve years old I wasn't the bravest kid in town, to tell the truth, I was scared of the dark. Or of things that crept around in the dark. I took the shotgun and an old five-gallon bucket to set on. As it got dark, I jumped at every strange noise I heard.

There was a piece of tin nailed over a window with a hole cut in it big enough for a stove pipe. We once had a wood stove out there to keep things warm. I was sitting real quiet listening to the turkeys and anything else that moved. Suddenly something hit the tin, and the mangiest old tom cat came crawling through the hole. I yanked back both hammers on the old shotgun, pointed it at the cat and let fly. Both barrels went off blowing the tin, cat, and all out into the turkey yard. It knocked me backward off the bucket. I dropped the shotgun, and just froze, laying there in the turkey crap and sawdust. I could hear Dad holler, "Did you get him, boy?"

Dad came busting through the door, hollering, "What in hell did you shoot?" I was so shaken I just pointed at the hole where the tin used to be. He said, "Boy, did you have to blow the hell out of everything?" I finally managed to speak a little. All I could say was it was a cat. "Well, he is a dam dead one now, there is cat hair, guts, and fur all over the place. What did you do to pull both triggers at the same time?" I broke open the old shotgun, and looked and both shells had been fired.

"That must have hurt, are you ok?" I just stood there like a dumb kid and grinned, as I rubbed my shoulder. Dad rubbed my hair and said, "It's a wonder it didn't blow you off the bucket." I laughed and said, "It did, I didn't roll in the turkey crap for fun." We both laughed, and Dad said, "We better nail something over the hole as you blew half the wall out." We put a piece of tin roofing over the hole. Checked on all the brooders and turkeys. And went to the house.

After I finally got to sleep, I would dream of the old cat coming through the hole, right at me. I would jump wide awake with my heart pounding.

The next morning, I walked out to the turkey shed to check on my marksmanship. I sure blew the heck out of everything, don't know what size shot was in that old twelve gauge but must have been number four or bigger. I got a shovel out of the shed and buried what was left of the old cat.

I could go on about a lot of my childhood adventures but don't want to bore you. I was just an average student in school. I never took a book home and studied like I should have, I had a sister a year ahead of me and she kept all her school papers so I usually studied what she saved, as it was the same book and same teacher. I had a B average in most classes, Math scared me so I didn't do very well in it. I never took Algebra and that came to hurt me when I got into electrical school in the Navy. I paid other men to teach me at night what I should have known.

I went into the Navy shortly after I got out of high school, I spent the summer working on a hay truck and worked at a gas station in Springfield where I tried to go to college on a football scholarship. That was an awakening, I had just turned seventeen the first of May and that was in August.

It didn't take long for me to realize I didn't belong there, some of the players were in their twenties, and they played for keeps.

So, I quit college, a friend and I decided to join the Marines. Thank God the Marine recruiter wasn't there that day, I joined the Navy and my friend went into the Air Force as he couldn't swim. My three brothers had all been in the Navy so kept up the family tradition.

I will never forget the first night in the Navy barracks. There were about forty other young men there with me. All of us were homesick and sorry for what we had done. Some of the boys were crying and really hurting. I just figured I had to stay in there for four years. So, I just sucked it up and tried to comfort them. We talked most of the night, and morning came quickly. We were marched to a chow hall and had breakfast. After that we were marched to a building full of doctors, and dentists, they made us strip off naked and give a physical. Afterward, we were given a pair of white shorts to wear. It was now the dentist's turn to see who they could make gag the loudest.

We then went into a supply room, were given a duffel bag, and marched down rows of stacked clothing where our uniforms, underwear, shoes, socks etc., were thrown to us. They made us count each item, and write it on a list they had given us, then we were told what items to put on and how to wear them. The rest we put into the duffle bag and wrote out the name on the bag.

It was lunchtime so they again march us to the chow hall and fed us a good lunch, except for the onion soup they tried to make me eat. It didn't happen. I refused and was made to do fifty pushups, and told to get the hell out of the mess hall.

After chow we went into another building, they had cut stencils for each of us. We were shown how to lay out all our clothing, and told to stencil our name on them in a certain place. This took most of the afternoon.

We put all our gear into a duffle bag and marched to another building and assigned a bunk. This was to be our barracks for the rest of the time we would be there. We had to take all the possession that we had brought with us. Civilian clothes, pictures, rings, shoes, etc. These we put in a box, sealed it and mailed it home.

The next morning, we were marched to the chow hall for breakfast. After that we had to go back to the barracks and wash all the clothes we were issued. This was done by hand on a table with soap and a scrub bush. We had to tie each item on a line with a short piece of string called clothes stop.

Each knot had to be a square knot that we were shown how to tie. Any clothes that were not tied properly were cut down, walked on, and you had to scrub them again. This took most of the day, so we were left to stay in the barracks and put away dry clothing. Showed how to fold it properly. So that it would fit into a locker about two-foot square.

The next morning, I was told to pack my bag with every item and report out front. I showed up along with several other men. We were told to go to a numbered barracks that was known as a holding company. We would stay there until we got dental work done.

They gave each of us a list as to what day and time we were to report to the dentist. The time I wasn't at the dentist, I was assigned to the chaplain's office, where I read and typed letters for the men that couldn't read or write. Some of them were very hard to read, but I did the best I could. I did this for over six weeks even after I had all my dental work finished. One day, the Chaplin asked me what school I was going to. I was assigned to Aviation election mate school. After I finished the basic, he asked when I would finish, and I told him I didn't know as I hadn't started yet.

He made a phone call, and a lieutenant showed up, and told me to pack my gear and go to a barracks and check with a petty officer named Waters.

They assigned me to a company that had been drilling for three weeks, heck I didn't know anything about marching, in step, about-face, or column left, or right. So, I missed lunch and another recruit took me out to the marching arena called a grinder, and he showed me a lot of stuff I couldn't remember. I know the drill instructor thought I was the dumbest hick he had ever instructed.

I got a lot of hollering at, and butt-chewing for a week or two, but finally got some of it right. After nine weeks of training, I got shipped to Norman Oklahoma, to a military prep school. I had spent seventeen weeks at Great Lakes when it should have been only nine weeks. After three months of prep school where we were shown all the basic jobs in the Navy, I was then shipped to Florida.

I hated Jacksonville. It rained every afternoon and the steam would come off the ground like fog. I had a rough time in school there, as I never took Algebra in high school. I paid guys to teach me at night, stuff that I should have had to take in high school. So being as I finished next to last in my class. I got shipped three buildings away to Naval Air Base, Jacksonville, Florida. And against all warning from friends, and officers, I volunteered for air crewman school. A week later I got a notice, I had been accepted, at last I was getting out of Jacksonville.

I was sent to Lakehurst, New Jersey, for parachute training and other air survival skills. After that I went to Adak, Alaska for a week of artic survival training. From there, we went to China Lake, California for a week of desert survival training then down to San Diego, California for water survival. Most of the training wasn't too bad except we didn't get much to eat. And the water training scared the crap out of me. Especially the Dilbert Dunker, which was part of an airplane on a track, that ran down to the bottom of a swimming pool and turned upside down. You had to open the canopy, unstrap yourself, get a parachute you were sitting on, and come to the surface without drowning. But it was worth it, when I got my air crewman wings, those I have always been very proud of.

I served aboard the aircraft carrier the USS Coral Sea, for fourteen months, made the 1956 Madeiran cruise, got to visit a lot of foreign countries and made the trip around the horn from Norfolk, Virginia to Bremerton, Washington, stopping in Chile, Brazil, and Panama. From there I was transferred to San Diego, California, to VRF 32 Squadron where I got to fly a lot. We were ferrying both old and new planes all across the United States. I loved that duty, and would have made a career of the Navy.

Except every two years you had to serve two years sea duty, and I didn't want to go back on a carrier. The flight deck and landings are a very dangerous place to be. My enlistment was up on April 30th 1959, I took it after a lot of consideration about making the Navy a career. I wanted to find a nice girl and get married and raise a family. I stayed in California and went to work for General Motors, making the 60 Chevrolets.

That December I got laid off during the changeover. After that, I went to work for a manufacturing plant called Torrington, where we made all kinds of fan blades. It was there I met a girl named Virginia Chose, she was from Montana, and just didn't fit into California any better than I did. I fell in love with her and we were married on April 22, 1961.

Virginia didn't want to live in Missouri, and I didn't want to live in Montana, because of the cold weather. So, we moved to Oregon where she had a brother living. I worked several jobs around Mill City. I worked for the Bureau of Land Management on a survey crew for several months, set chockers for a month for a logging company. That job kept me so scared; I was looking for another one all the time.

I went to work for Simpson plywood mill, for most of a year, then took a carpenter job with Mill City Builders. Virginia was pregnant, and our son Stephen was born on February 22, 1963. I had been an electrician in the Navy. One day I was in the highway building in Salem. I just happened to see a notice on their bulletin board they were looking for an electrician's helper. We were working on the last house we had to build so I applied for the job and got hired.

I was sent to Grants Pass on June the first in 1963. We drove down with everything we owned in the back seat and trunk of an old 41 Cadillac.

As luck would have it, we arrived just as the Boatnik parade was starting, and the town was full of people. But God was with us and we found a furnished guest house for rent. It was a nice clean little house, with a large living room, nice kitchen, and a good-sized bedroom. It was only about five blocks from where I was to work.

The first day there I found out that it was a traveling job, we covered eight counties in southern Oregon. I didn't really like leaving Virginia and Steve alone in a strange town, but had to have a job. I liked the electrical work, except for the high radio towers and light poles we had to climb. We spent the first week in Klamath Falls, then Eugene, Roseburg and Coos Bay, every fifth week we stayed in Grants Pass. We got home on Friday nights most of the time. I was on call so got called out a lot to fix traffic signal problems on weekends.

We grew to really like Grants Pass, I spent sixteen years as a volunteer fireman and fought a lot of hot fires for the city. I also spent eight years as a city reserve police officer, I liked doing that but Virginia didn't like me being gone all the time, and I don't blame her.

We had another addition to our family on May 23, 1965 when our daughter Rhonda was born. Our children grew up way too fast. Both of them have done well in life. And have raised families of their own and now have grandchildren.

I retired from my electrical job with the state in 1995 after 34 years, and I still live in Grants Pass. Virginia finally got tired of me after I retired, and we divorced in February 2011. We are still friends and have each made a life of our own. She now lives in Idaho, as do both of our children.

I can't say I have had the best life, but it has been damn interesting, and most of the time life has been good to me. I have been in 46 of the 50 states, all over Europe and visited all the coastal countries of South America, and Mexico made a trip around the horn of Antarctica and sailed both the Pacific and Atlantic oceans. Crossed the Equator, International Date Line, been to Guam, Philippines, Japan, Wake Island, and Tonkin Bay off Viet Nam. I was born and raised in Walnut Grove, Missouri. A place and people I will always love. They called me David when I was young, as Mom wanted me to be a preacher. I am ordained but don't consider myself a minister.

Joseph Murray Keen
Birth: 27 February 1840
Bridgeton, Cumberland, New Jersey
Death: 17 March 1920
Ash Grove, Greene, Missouri
  Susan Lamar
  Birth: about 1845
  Campbell, Tennessee
  Death: about 1893
  Greene, Missouri
Marriage: 4 April 1866
Children:
   1.) Margaret "Marietta" Keen (1843 - 5/26/1861)
   2.) William Keen (9/21/1867 - Deceased)
   3.) John Keen (10/15/1868 - about 1869)
   4.) Margaret Keen (1869 - Deceased)
   5.) Albert Keen (4/25/1871 - 3/7/1915)
   6.) Malissa Jane Keen (12/18/1872 - about 1886)
   7.) Charles Erwin Keen (7/3/1874 - 6/22/1964)
   8.) Oliver Walter Keen (10/10/1877 - 2/11/1947)
   9.) Sarah Alice Keen (Feb 1879 - Deceased)
  10.) Joseph Harve Keen (3/14/1881 - 2/20/1962)
  11.) Mary Louanna Keen (10/8/1883 - 7/19/1959)
  12.) Thomas Wilburn Keen (10/8/1883 - 4/18/1972)

Mary Elizabeth Hammet
Birth: 28 September 1844
Birmingham Township, Chester, Pennsylvania
Death: 17 January 1915
Ash Grove, Greene, Missouri

Mary Keen and Joseph Murray Keen

Charles Erwin Keen and Dollie Jane Keen

Great-grandfather Joseph Keen. As the information I have, Joseph Keen came here from New Jersey to the state of Missouri. Date unknown.

Susan (Lamar) Keen and twins

Cherokee Census of ALABAMA – 1935

<u>Heads of Families</u>

OF MORGAN CITY
Five Killers
Coltanst
Dick-all-string
Parch Corn Flower
Toon-i-ah

OF BLOUNT CITY
Doniel Spencer
Corn Silk
Robert Lovett
Widow Monk
Samuel Neal
Hugh Henry
L.D. Parrot
Richard Fields
Dawson Cheek
Saul-de-kee
Captain Boldridge
David Carter
Alexander Gilbreath
Martin Schrimaher
Speaker
E. Thompson
John Bell
Robert Brown
Kal-sow-uee
Ooh-lah ne tah tah
Young Puppy
Johnewanah
Barry Hughes
Joseph Crutchfield
Sonkier
Roasting Bear
Rising Fawn
Bark Flule
Scraper
Kah-tlanah-cha
Antooyes skie

<u>Heads of Families</u>

Rider Fields
John G. Ross
Kah-ka-takh
Chu-wee
Man Killer
John Boote
Ta-tah-seh-hah
James Lamar
George Baldridge
Ooh-lone-stes-kee
Jas-oor
Tuh-nal-ak-oh
Schreech Owl
Betsy Broom
H. Buckingham
White Tobacco

FT. ARMSTRONG
Watta
Ali-cho-nah
Head Thrower
Te-yeh-tis-kee
Atwatta Big Belly
Grittee
Charles Doening
Corn Tassel
Jackson Mankiller
Chu-coa-quoh
An-neck-ah yale te her
Cilcy

OF LITTLE RIVER
Two Fathom
William Grimmett
Culsh-yeh
Chow-es-kee
Eustee
Crying Snake
Oo-lah-neah-tak

Levi H. Keen - Lebanon, MO – 1896

Phenix Store

Joseph Harve Keen
Birth: 14 March 1881
Birthplace: Bolivar, Polk, Missouri
Married: 2 August 1903
Death: 20 February 1962
Mother: Susan Lamar
Father: Joseph Murray Keen
Joseph Harve married **Anna Valina Alberta Elizabeth Brady**
    Anna Valina Alberta Elizabeth Brady
    Birth: 20 May 1885
    Birthplace: Boone Township, Greene Missouri
    Death: 20 April 1967
    Mother: Maryland Parthenia Kerr
    Father: John Aaron Brady, Jr.
Children of Joseph Harve and Anna Valina:
   13.) Hershel (9/23/1904 - Deceased)
   14.) Albert Carl (11/19/1905 - 12/29/1969)
   15.) Gladys Marie (11/7/1907 - 1/25/1970)
   16.) Willie (6/18/1910 - 6/23/1910)
   17.) Esther May (5/13/1911 - 5/30/2008)
   18.) Joseph Arol (11/12/1913 - 7/18/1969)
   19.) Sterling Emulus (3/14/1917 - 2/4/1977)
   20.) Gene Smith (3/14/1917 - 7/12/2012)
   21.) Virginia Pauline (1/4/1921 - 6/6/2014)
   22.) John Wilburn (11/23/1923 - 5/1/1994)

Joseph Harve Keen and Anna Valina Elizabeth (Brady) Keen

Joseph, Anna, Carl, and Marie Keen

Albert Carl Keen
Birth: 19 November 1905
Death: 29 December 1969
Albert Carl Keen married **Myrtle Olive Grant**

   Myrtle Olive Grant
   Birth: 28 November 1906
   Death: 2 March 1992
   Mother: Mary A. Mullins
   Father: Elmes Cathes Grant
Children of Albert Carl and Myrtle Olive:
   1.) Vera Lee Keen (28 Aug 1925 - 1 Aug 2016)
   2.) Joanna Lou Keen (14 June 1927 - 17 Feb 2018)
   3.) Albert Harve Keen (30 Jan 1929 - 26 Nov 2009)
   4.) Muriel Don Keen (2 March 1933 - 18 June 2020)

Carl and **Myrtle** divorced around 1934.

Albert Carl married **Ruby Maude (Poole) McCullough** on 24 May 1935
   Ruby Maude McCullough
   Birth: 16 May 1907
   Death: 27 April 1962
Ruby had two children by first marriage:
   1.) Marvin Russell (11 Nov 1932 - 16 March 1984)
   2.) Evelyn Nell (14 Feb 1934 - 26 March 2011)

Children of Carl and Ruby:
1.) Nancy Sue (15 Feb 1936 - 16 March 1990)
2.) Karl David (born 1 May 1938)
3.) Sally Juanita (born 9 Nov 1940)
4.) Barbara Kay (19 Dec 1941 - 20 Jan 1985)
5.) Phyllis Jean (born 12 Aug 1943)
6.) Cynthia Ann (7 Jan 1949 - 2 May 2007)

After Carl and Myrtle divorced, she married Otis Keen. Myrtle and Otis divorced; Myrtle then married Leonard Hopper. Myrtle Leonard had no children together. No dates on either of the marriages.

Otis Wilburn Keen
Birth: 30 March 1907
Death: 26 Dec 1976
Mother: Alice M. Jackson (23 May 1887 - 3 April 1955)
Father: Thomas W. Keen (8 Oct 1883 - 18 April 1972)

Vera Lee Keen
Born: 28 Aug 1925
Birthplace: Phenix MO, Greene Co
Married: 16 Aug 1946
Mother: Myrtle Olive Grant
Father: Albert Carl Keen
Vera Lee married **James Kern Hinkle**
Vera Lee was a registered nurse in the Cadet Nurse Corp during WWII.

   James Bern Hinkle
   Born: 6 Dec 1923
   James lived in Polk Co most of his life
      Death: 2 May 1999
      Mother: Ruth M. (Kern) Hinkle
      Father: Wade Hinkle
      James served in the 738th Tank Battalion during WWII first army.

Children of Vera Lee and James:
   1.) **Robert Dean Hinkle**
      Born: 27 Aug 1950
      Birthplace: Springfield MO
      Lived in Polk Co.
      Married: 12 June 1992
      Robert Dean married **Linda Ann Bogad**

Linda Ann Bogad
Born: 11 April 1965
Mother: Joan Ellen (Dickman) Bogad
Father: Michael Eugene Bogad Sr.
Robert Dean taught school.

2.) **Norma Lea Hinkle**
Born: 12 Dec 1953
Birthplace: Springfield MO
Norma Lea married **Gregory Lynn May**

   Gregory Lynn May
   Born: 28 March 1950
   Birthplace: Stone Co, MO
   Mother: Mary Lucille Logan May
   Father: Orville Ralph May Jr.
Children of Norma Lea and Gregory Lynn:
   1.) **James Gregory May**
      Born: 13 Sept 1983
      James played the French horn with the 135 National Guard Band in Springfield MO since his Jr. year of high school.
   2.) **Leigha Lynn May**
      Born: 13 Oct 1987
      Leigha plays the flute with the Southwest Missouri Children's Center.

Joanna Lou Keen
Born: 14 June 1927
Birthplace: Phenix MO
Joanna married **Gray Wilson** in California
Children of Joanna and Gray:
  1.) **Julie Wilson**
      Julie married **Donald Wendt** in California
      Children of Julie and Donald:
        1.) Grant Wendt
        2.) Wade Wendt
        3.) Ashley Wendt

Joanna married **Robert Scott**
Children of Joanna and Robert:
  1.) **Jo Lynn Scott**
      Born: 17 Sept 1953
      Birthplace: Juneau, Alaska
      Jo Lynn married **Curt Albert; Jo Lynn** and **Curt** had no children.
      Jo Lynn married **Russell Alan Kruse; Jo Lynn** and **Russell Alan** have two boys.

Joanna married **Roland Samson**
Children of Joanna and Roland:
  1.) **Cathy Samson**
      Married: 21 June 1984
      Cathy Samson married **James Jacobsmeier**
      Children of Cathy and James:
        1.) Veronica Jacobsmeier

Cathy was married a second time and had no children.

Albert Harve Keen
Born: 30 January 1929
Mother: Myrtle Olive Grant
Father: Albert Carl Keen
Albert Harve Keen married **Patricia Lee**

   Patricia Lee
   Born: 13 June 1927
   Children of Albert Harve Keen and Patricia Lee:
      1.) **Nancy Kay Keen** (born 11 Jan 1949)
       Nancy Kay Keen married **William (Bill) Edwards**
       Children of Nancy and William:
         1.) Zachary Albert Edwards

      2.) **Sharon Lee Keen** (born 27 May 1952)
       Sharon had a twin brother that died soon after birth.
       Married: 9 Oct 1972 Salem, Oregon
       Sharon Lee Keen married **Steven M. Hoeye**
       Children of Sharon and Steven:
         1.) Melinda Ann Hoeye
         2.) Erin Brook Hoeye

      3.) **Susan Keen** (born 23 March 1953)
       Susan Keen married **Thomas I Chamblee**
       Children of Susan and Thomas:
         1.) Dustin Eugene Chamblee
         2.) Daniel Issac Chamblee

Muriel Don Keen
Born: 2 March 1933
Birthplace: Green Co, Phenix MO
Married: 28 May 1952
Mother: Myrtle Olive Grant
Father: Albert Carl Keen
Muriel Don Keen married **Wanda Ruth Wiles**
  Wanda Ruth Wiles
  Born: 10 Aug 1935
  Mother: Tennessee McCormac (born 8 June 1913)
  Father: Raymond Wiles (born 8 Aug 1904)
Children of Don and Wanda:
  1.) **Dwight Alan Keen** (born 17 Nov 1954)
    Married: 18 Aug 1973
      Dwight Alan married **Edna Christine Pendergrass**
      Edna Christine Pendergrass
      Born: 15 Dec 1955
      Birthplace: Pleasant Hope MO
    Children of Dwight Alan and Christine:
      1.) **Leland Grant Keen** (born 27 Nov 1979)
      Leland Grant married **Kelly Wolf**
      Kelly Wolf had one child before she married
      Leland Grant
        1.) Annalissa Marie Wolf (born 24 May 2000)
        Children of Leland and Kelly:
        1.) Morgan Paige Keen (born 27 Jan 2004)
      2.) **Amanda Grace Keen** (born 25 Aug 1982)
    Dwight Alan divorced in 2002 and married a 2nd time.
    Dwight Alan and **Raynell** married 12 June 2004.
  2.) **Donna Ruth Keen** (born 1 Sept 1963)
    Married: 16 July 1982, Brighton MO
    Donna Ruth Keen married **Teddy Dean Pridgen**
      Teddy Dean Pridgen (born 12 June 1962)
    Children of Donna Ruth and Teddy Dean
      1.) Lisa Elaine Pridgen (born 17 Aug 1987)
    Donna Ruth divorced in 1997 and married a 2nd time.

Donna Ruth married **Jerry Leon Basinger** 15 Sept 2001
Jerry Leon Basinger
Born: 26 March 1946
Birthplace: West Plains, MO
Mother: Ida Mae Baxter
Father: Orval John Basinger

Marvin Russell McCullough Keen
Born: 12 Nov 1932
Married: 7 Dec 1957
Death: 16 March 1984
Mother: Ruby Maude (Poole) McCullough
Marvin Russell married **Ruth Evans**
   Ruth Evans (died Oct 1992)
Children of Marvin Russell and Ruth:
   1.) Rickey Albert (born 3 Dec 1958)
   2.) Linda Evelyn (born 13 Oct 1960)
   3.) Penny Ann (born 21 Jan 1965)
   4.) Diane (born 21 June 1967)

Evelyn Nell McCullough
Born: 14 Feb 1934
Married: 7 May 1951
Mother: Ruby Maude (Poole) McCullough
Evelyn Nell married **Clyde Earl Smith**
Children of Evelyn Nell and Clyde Earl Smith:
    1.) Gary Clyde (born 9 July 1952)
    2.) Rita Ann (born 29 Sept 1953)
    3.) Debra Lynn (born 18 April 1957)
    4.) Bradly Earl (born 21 March 1962)
Evelyn and **Clyde** divorced Aug 1961.
Evelyn married **Warren Dale Garrison** 6 April 1979; They
divorced about 2002.

Nancy Sue Keen
Born: 15 Feb 1936
Married: May 1955
Death: 16 March 1990
Mother: Ruby Maude (Poole) McCullough
Father: Albert Carl Keen
Nancy Sue married **Robert Sebring**
  Robert Sebring (died 10 Sept 1964)
Children of Nancy Sue and Robert:
    1.) Bobbie Kim Sebring (born 4 June 1957)
    2.) Terrie Ruby Sebring (born 4 Oct 1962)
       { Twins }
    3.) Todd Ray Sebring (born 4 Oct 1962)

Karl David Keen
Born: 1 May 1938
Married: 22 April 1961
Mother: Ruby Maude (Poole) McCullough
Father: Albert Carl Keen
Karl David married **Virginia Chose**
Children of Karl David and Virginia:
    1.) Steven Carl (born 22 Feb 1963)
    2.) Ronda Renee (born 23 May 1965)

Sally Juanita Keen
Born: 9 Nov 1940
Married: 10 Sept 1957
Mother: Ruby Maude (Poole) McCullough
Father: Carl Albert Keen
Sally Juanita married **Delbert Graves**
Children of Sally Juanita and Delbert:
    1.) Jerry Leon (born 6 Feb 1962, stillborn)
    2.) Brian David (born 24 Sept 1963, stillborn)
    3.) Kenneth Paul Sartin (born 29 Sept 1964, adopted from Barbara Kay Keen)
    4.) Kerrie Lynn (born 23 Jan 1967)
    5.) Karla Kay (born 25 Feb 1970)
    6.) Kurtis Del (born 22 June 1972)

Barbara Kay Keen
Born: 19 Dec 1941
Married: 16 Jan 1958
Death: 20 Jan 1985
Mother: Ruby Maude (Poole) McCullough
Father: Albert Carl Keen
Barbara Kay married **Gary Sartin**
Children of Barbara Kay and Gary:
    1.) Carl Allen (born 9 April 1958)
    2.) David Gavin (born 15 July 1959)
    3.) Lisa Kay (born 29 May 1960)
    4.) Kenneth Paul (born 29 Sept 1961)
    5.) Charles Keith (born 15 Feb 1963)
    6.) Juanita Ann (born 10 Dec 1965)
Kay and **Gary** divorced; **Kay** married **David Bozman** 12 Sept 1966.
Children of Kay and David:
    1.) William Anthony (born 12 Dec 1968)

Phyllis Jean Keen
Born: 12 Aug 1943
Mother: Ruby Maude (Poole) McCullough
Father: Albert Carl Keen
Phyllis Jean married **Robert McNabb**
Children of Phyllis and Robert:
  1.) Robert Douglas (born 12 Aug 1960)
  2.) Jill Renee (born 10 Jan 1967)
  3.) Johnnie Albert (born 30 April 1970)
  4.) Karl James (born 3 March 1973)
Phyllis and **Bob** divorced 23 Sept 1975.
Phyllis married **James Emmett Thatcher** 3 March 1978.

Cynthia Ann Keen
Born: 7 Jan 1949
Married: 27 Dec 1967
Mother: Ruby Maude (Poole) McCullough
Father: Albert Carl Keen
Cynthia Ann married **Larry Wayne Hicks**
Children of Cynthia and Larry:
  1.) Larry W. (born 30 Dec 1968)
  2.) Wesley Scott (born 30 Jan 1971)
  3.) Ruby Ann (born 30 Sept 1972)
Cynthia and **Larry** divorced 9 April 1972.
Larry was killed in a car train accident.
Cynthia married **Frank Bell** Dec 1976.
Children of Cynthia and Frank:
  1.) David Russell (born Aug 22 ?)

Frank had two or three children, from a previous marriage, when he and **Cynthia** married.

Gladys Marie Keen (sister to **Carl Keen**)
Born: 7 Nov 1907
Married: 12 Oct 1925
Death: 25 Jan 1970
Buried: Greene Lawn, Walnut Grove
Mother: Anna Valina Alberta Elizabeth Brady
Father: Joseph Harve Keen
Gladys Marie Keen married **Charles J. Higman**
    Charles J. Higman
    Born: 14 July 1904
    Death: 26 Aug 1991
    Buried: Younger Cemetery near Stockton, MO
Children of Gladys and Charles:
    1.) Iva Jean (born 20 Aug 1926 in Lowery City)
    2.) Charles Dean (born 11 July 1928 in Phenix, MO)
    3.) Robert Lowell (born 23 April 1930, died 1 Sept 1933 in Phenix, MO)
    4.) Ron Keen (born 23 March 1933 in Greene Co, MO)
    5.) June Ann (born 21 June 1935 in Walnut Grove, MO)

Marie and **Charlie** divorced.

Marie married **Don Franks**
    Don Franks
    Born: 1 Sept 1910 in Poplar Bluff, MO
    Married: 20 Feb 1938
    Death: 16 Oct 1977 in Springfield, MO
    Buried: Greene Lawn Cemetery Walnut Grove, MO
Children of Marie and Don Franks:
    1.) Donna Sue Franks (born 21 Sept 1940)

Joseph Arol Keen (brother to Carl Keen)
Born: 12 Nov 1913
Birthplace: Greene Co, MO
Death: 18 July 1969
Buried: Greene Lawn Cemetery Walnut Grove, MO
Mother: Anna Valina Alberta Elizabeth Brady
Father: Joseph Naive Keen
Joseph Arol Keen married **Mildred Prevo**
   Mildred Prevo
   Born: 4 Sept 1912
   Death: 29 Jan 1940
   Buried: Greene Lawn Cemetery Walnut Grove, MO
Children of Joseph and Mildred:
   1.) Loren (born 1932 or 1933?)

Joe married **June Coker** and they had no children together.

Joe married **Ruby Davies**
Children of Joe and Ruby:
   1.) Katy Ann (born 29 Oct 1952, died 29 Oct 1952, buried
      in Walnut Grove Cemetery)
   2.) Jackie Lorene (born 19 Jan 1954)
   3.) Judy Ann (born 1 Oct 1956)

Gene Smith Keen (brother **to Carl Keen**; Twin to **Sterling Emulus Keen**)
Born: 14 March 1917
Birthplace: Phenix, MO
Married: 13 Dec 1938 in Mt. Vernon, MO
Mother: Anna Valina Alberta Elizabeth Brady
Father: Joseph Harve Keen
Gene Smith married **Virginia Ethel Stanton** of Ash Grove, MO
　　Virginia Ethel Stanton (born 19 Dec 1917)
Children of Gene and Virginia:
　　1.) Bobby Gene (born 18 Sept 1940 Springfield, MO, died 8 Dec 1943, buried 11 Dec 1943 Ash Grove, MO)
　　2.) Vickie Lea (born 6 Feb 1947 Springfield, MO, died 9 Dec 1956, buried Ash Grove Cemetery)

Sterling Emulus Keen (brother to **Carl Keen**; Twin to **Gene Smith Keen**)
Born: 14 March 1917
Death: 4 Feb 1977
Buried: Green lawn North Springfield, MO
Mother: Anna Valina Alberta Elizabeth Brady
Father: Joseph Harve Keen
Sterling Emulus married **Juanita Andrews**
No Children

Sterling married **Mildred Long**
Children of Sterling and Mildred Long:
　　1.) Richard Marion (Richey) (born 26 July 1946)

Mildred had two children by her first marriage:
　　1.) Linda
　　2.) Ann

Virginia Pauline Keen
Born: 4 Jan 1921
Married: 23 Sept 1939
Mother: Anna Valina Alberta Elizabeth Brady
Father: Joseph Harve Keen
Virginia married **Pacifico Jiz**
Children of Virginia and Pacifico:
1.) **Patricia Marilyn** (born 20 Jan 1942)
Patricia Marilyn married **Billy Hayter**
Children of Patricia and Billy:
1.) Todd Kendall (born 2 Aug 1961)
2.) Tea Nicole (born 31 Oct 1969)
2.) **Pamela Jo** (born 2 May 1942)
Pamela Jo married **James (Jim) Swearngin**
Children of Pamela and Jim:
1.) Jamie Jo (born 2 Jan 1964)
3.) **Michael Preston** (born 25 Feb 1954)
Michael Preston married **Cathy Cosby**
Children of Michael and Cathy:
1.) Jennifer (born 8 Dec 1997)

Pauline and **Pacifico** divorced.
Pauline married **Lano Pursley** in 4 Feb 1970.
Lano had four children by his first marriage:
1.) Lana
2.) Ruth
3.) Steve
4.) Neva

John Wilburn Keen (brother to Carl Keen)
Born: 23 Nov 1923
Married: 13 Sept 1942
Mother: Anna Valina Alberta Elizabeth Brady
Father: Joseph Harve Keen
   John Wilburn married **Anna Key** (born 27 June 1924)
Children of John and Anna:
   1.) **John Willett** (born 4 Dec 1944)
      Married: July 1964
      John Willett married **Janet McGill**
      John and Janet had no children and they divorced.
      John married **Berta Phumphery**
      Berta had one child from her previous marriage. **John**
      adopted this child.
         1.) Keith Allen (born 9 July 1966)
      Children of John and Berta:
         1.) Anna Lucretia (born 26 Oct 1971)
   2.) **Susan Grace** (born 11 Dec 1950)
      Married: 28 April 1969
      Susan **Grace** married **Richard Wayne McKinney**
      Children of Susan and Richard:
         1.) Kimberly Dawn (born 6 Feb 1970)
      Susan and **Richard** divorced.
      Susan married **James Cameron Blake Cloyd**
         James Cameron Blake Cloyd (born: 20 June 1931)
         Birthplace: St. Louis, MO
         Married: 30 June 1972
      Susan and **James** had no children together, but **James**
      adopted **Kimberly Dawn McKinney** in 1986.
   3.) **William Timothy** (born 17 March 1956)
      Married: 25 Jan 1986
      William **Timothy** married **Carol Faith Mason**
         Carol Faith Mason (born 16 April 1944)
         Death: 20 Aug 1990
         Carol had 2 or 3 children from previous marriages.
         Children names and birthdates are unknown.

Charles (Uncle Charley) Keen (brother to Joseph Harve)
Born: 7 March 1874
Death: 22 June 1964
Mother: Susan Lamar
Father: Joseph Murray Keen
Charles Keen married **Dollie Jane Willis**
   Dollie Jane Willis
   Born: 1 May 1881
   Death: 24 Feb 1964
Children of Charles and Dollie:
   1.) **Virgil Leslie** (born 13 Nov 1902)
      Died: 27 May 1980
      Buried: Porterville, CA
   2.) **Mae**
   3.) **Lawrence Desmon** (born 7 July 1909)
      Died: 1 Feb 1975
      Buried: Bakersfield, CA
   4.) **Orther** (born 10 Nov 1908, stillborn)
   5.) **Glen** (born 5 Apr 1910, stillborn)
   6.) **Gladys Wilma** (born 30 Sept 1911)
      Died: Oct 1993
   7.) **Cliffy** (girl) (born 24 Aug 1919)
      Died: 1 March 1921
      Buried: Greene Lawn Cemetery Walnut Grove, MO
   8.) **Alice Ruth** (born 25 July 1924)
      Died: ?
      Alice was cremated; Her ashes were scattered from a plane.

Virgil Leslie
Born: 13 Nov 1902
Death: 27 May 1980
Mother: Dollie Jane Willis
Father: Charles Keen
Virgil Leslie married **Mae Bodenhames**
  Mae Bodenhames (born 6 Feb 1905)
  Death: 3 Feb 1931
Children of Virgil and Mae:
    1.) **Frances** (born 5 April 1922)
       Died: 23 April 1934
       Buried: Green Lawne Cemetery Walnut Grove, MO
    2.) **Myrtle Bell** (born 27 March 1926 in CA)
    3.) **Charles** (born 3 Feb 1921)

Virgil Leslie married **Nora Brown**
Nora Brown had a son named **Eugene.**
Virgil and **Nora** had several children including two sets of twins. Not all of the children's names are known. The two that are known are **Leslie Ray** and **Aretta**, and **Don** and **Lou Alma Lee.**

Gladys Wilma Keen
Born: 30 Sept 1911
Death: Oct 1993
Mother: Dollie Jane Willis
Father: Charles Keen
Gladys Wilma married **John Nibler**
Children of Gladys and John:
1.) Betty Jo (born 7 May 1932)
2.) Kenneth Leroy (born 1 Oct 1933?)
3.) Marion Dale (born Nov or Dec 1934)
Marion died at just a few weeks old.

Gladys married **Clarence Tuck**
Clarence Tuck
Married: 17 May 1937
Clarence had two daughters.
1.) Thelma Lorene Tuck (born 7 Aug 1928)
2.) Anna Mae Tuck (born 3 March 1930)

Children of Gladys and Clarence:
1.) Arthur Wayne Tuck (born 16 Aug 1940)

Walter Keen (brother of **Joseph Harve Keen**)
Born: 10 Oct 1877
Death: 11 Feb 1947
Mother: Susan Lamar
Father: Joseph Murray Keen
Walter married **Nora Josephine Cawthorn**
    Nora Josephine Cawthorn
    Born: 9 March 1885
    Death: 15 April 1913
No children.

Walt married **Clara G. Wallace**
    Clara G. Wallace
    Born: 14 July 1892
    Death: 25 Jan 1978
Children of Walt and Clara:
    1.) Glynn (born 18 June 1916)
        Died: 2 Nov 1916
    2.) Floyd Murray (born 9 Oct 1923)
        Died: 20 Dec 2003
        Buried: Ash Grove Cemetery

Mary Louanna Keen (twin sister to **Thomas W. Keen**) (sister to **Joseph Harve Keen**)
Born: 8 Oct 1883
Birthplace: Polk Co, MO
Married: 1 Dec 1901
Death: 19 July 1959
Buried: Ash Grove, MO
Mother: Susan Lamar
Father: Joseph Murray Keen
Mary Louanna married **James Emery Brady**
    James Emery Brady
    Born: 17 May 1877
    Death: 29 Aug 1960
Children of Mary Louanna and James:
1.) Charles Edward (born 16 Aug 1902, died 21 Dec 1945, buried Wichita KS)
   Married: 1992 to Phoebe Getters in El Dondo, KS
2.) Joseph Raymond (born 12 July 1904 in Phenix, MO, died 13 April 1976)
   Married: 3 April 1924 to Lillian Beatrice Martin
3.) Lester Eugene (born 20 Jan 1907 in Phenix, MO, died 2 May 1980 Corvina CA)
   Married: 1 Sept 1927 to Arrilee Grantham in Phenix, MO
4.) Millard Emery (born 19 May 1909 in Phenix, MO)
   Married: 22 Nov 1927 to Lucy Gaines in Phenix, MO
5.) Susan Irene Brady (born 25 July 1911 in Phenix, MO, died 14 Feb 1984 Justin, CA)
   Married: 6 April 1929 to Victor Cates
6.) Ona Lucille Brady (born about 6 Oct 1913 in Carthage, MO)
   Married: about 1935 to Wayne Rummel
7.) Vera Ella Brady (born 28 Feb 1917, died Nov 1973 El Monte, CA)
   Married: Charles Hurd; Divorced
8.) Jessie Lee Brady (born 6 July 1919)
   Married: 17 Feb 1940 to Farris H. Brown

9.) Betty Ann Brady (born 10 July 1921)
Married: Gene Bacon; divorced
Remarried a man by the last name of Ramsey; possibility
of two daughters.

Thomas (Uncle Tom) Wiburn Keen (brother to **Joseph Harve Keen**)
Born: 8 Oct 1883
Death: 18 April 1972
Buried: Greene Lawn Cemetery Walnut Grove, MO
Mother: Susan Lamar
Father: Joseph Murray Keen
Thomas Wilburn married **Alice (Allie) Jackson**
Alice (Allie) Jackson
Born: 23 May 1887
Death: 18 April 1955
Buried: Greene Lawn Cemetery Walnut Grove, MO
Children of Thomas and Alice:
1.) Otis Wilburn (born 30 March 1907, died 26 Dec 1976)
2.) Velma (born 29 Sept 1908, died 4 June 2006)
3.) Ella Leona (born 9 Oct 1910, died 27 March 1986)
4.) Leonard Leon (born 14 March 1913, died 28 April 1995)
5.) Edna L. (born 3 Oct 1915, died 3 Jan 1992)
6.) Vivian (born 24 Sept, died 8 Dec 1920)
7.) Kenneth Len (born 1 Jan 1921)
8.) Howard Lee (born 5 June 1923)
9.) Gordon Wayne (born 31 July 1926, died 13 April 1984)
10.) Nina Mae (born 15 Nov 1931)

Velma Keen
Born: 29 Sept 1908
Mother: Alice Jackson
Father: Thomas Wilburn Keen
Velma married **Glen A. Oaley**
    Glen A. Oaley
    Born: 2 Nov 1902
    Death: 15 Sept 1983
Children of Velma and Glen:
    1.) Patsy
    2.) James
    3.) Robert

Edna L. Keen
Born: 3 Oct 1915
Death: 3 Jan 1992
Buried: Greene Lawn Cemetery Walnut Grove, MO
Mother: Alice Jackson
Father: Thomas Wilburn Keen
Edna married **Leo Witt**
    Leo Witt
    Born: 13 Oct 1910
    Death: 31 Jan 1994
Children of Edna and Leo:
    1.) Norma Lorene (married Don Butler)
    2.) Peggy Nadine (born 27 Oct 1936, died 1 Dec 1936, buried Greene Lawn Cemetery Walnut Grove, MO)
    3.) Linda Christine (born 18 Sept 1937, infant death, buried Green Lawn Cemetery Walnut Grove, MO)
    4.) Larry Dean (born 18 Jan 1939, died 1939)
    5.) Teddy Theodore (born 24 May 1941)
    6.) Jerry Lynn (born 1 Jan 1946)

Linda Kay
Married: about 2 Jan 1970
Linda Kay married **Donald David Cheffey**
Children of Linda and Donald:
   1.) David Eugene (born 15 Nov 1970)
Linda and **Donald David** divorced; she then married **Donald Ray Wright. Linda** and **Donald Ray** had no children together and they divorced.

Gary Len
Married: 27 Dec 1971
Gary Len married **Barbara Jean Jewell**
   Barbara Jean Jewell
   Born: 17 Sept 1952
Children of Gary and Barbara:
   1.) Scotty Len (born 25 April 1972 in Louisiana)
   2.) Correy Dale (born 18 May 1975 in Homestead, FL)
Gary and **Barbara** divorced; he then married **Rhonda**. She had one son by her first husband.

Kenneth Len Keen
Born: 1 Jan 1921
Married: 20 Aug 1946
Mother: Alice Jackson
Father: Thomas Wilburn Keen
Kenneth Len married **Margie Gibson**
Margie Gibson
Born: 25 Nov 1925
Children of Kenneth and Margie:
   1.) Linda Kay (born 17 May 1948)
   2.) Kenneth Leon (only lived for a few hours)
   3.) Gary Len (born 10 Sept 1951)